One State, Two States

One State, Two States

Resolving the Israel/Palestine Conflict

Benny Morris

YALE UNIVERSITY PRESS   NEW HAVEN & LONDON

Set in Janson Text type by Integrated Publishing Solutions.
Printed in the United States of America.

Library of Congress Cataloging-in-Publication Data
Morris, Benny, 1948–
One state, two states : resolving the Israel/Palestine conflict / Benny Morris.
p. cm.
Includes bibliographical references and index.
ISBN 978-0-300-12281-7 (clothbound : alk. paper)
1. Arab-Israeli conflict—Peace.   2. Israel-Arab War, 1948–1949—Influence.
3. Israel-Arab War, 1948–1949—Causes.   4. Jewish-Arab relations—History—
1947–1948.   5. Palestinian Arabs—Politics and government.   6. Palestine—
Politics and government—1917–1948.   7. Israel—Politics and government.
8. Zionism—History. I. Title.
DS119.7.M6565 2009
956.9405'4—dc22   2008040285

A catalogue record for this book is available from the British Library.

This paper meets the requirements of ANSI/NISO
Z39.48–1992 (Permanence of Paper).
It contains 30 percent postconsumer waste (PCW)
and is certified by the Forest Stewardship Council (FSC).

10 9 8 7 6 5 4 3 2 1

Contents

ACKNOWLEDGMENTS vii

MAPS viii

LIST OF ABBREVIATIONS xv

1 The Reemergence of One-Statism 1

2 The History of One-State and Two-State Solutions 28

3 Where To? 161

NOTES 203

BIBLIOGRAPHY 223

INDEX 230

Acknowledgments

I would like to thank Professors Beni Kedar, Ruth Gavison, and Ron Zweig, as well as the anonymous readers, for reading and commenting on the manuscript. Their suggestions and corrections have added much to the quality of the outcome.

I would like to thank Jeff Abel for, as usual, sorting out various technical issues.

My thanks, too, to Georges Borchardt and Jonathan Brent for making the book possible and to Laura Jones Dooley for helping fashion the outcome.

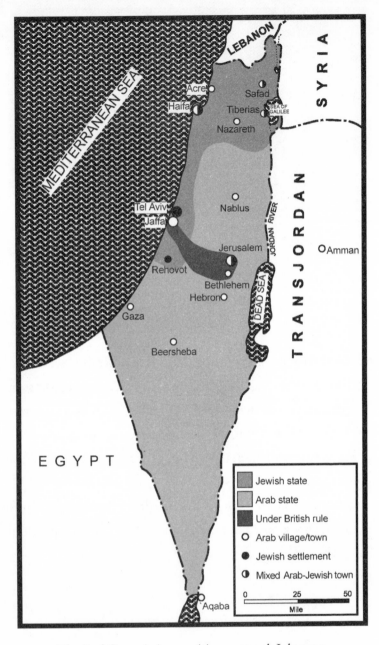

The Peel Commission partition proposal, July 1937.

The UN General Assembly partition proposal, November 1947.

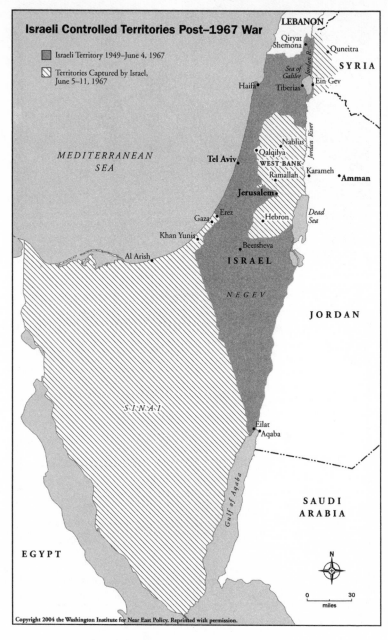

Israel and the Occupied Territories, 11 June 1967.

The Allon Plan, 1967–1968.

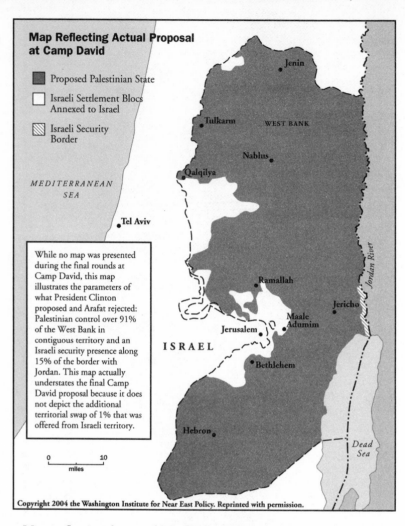

Map Reflecting Actual Proposal at Camp David

Proposed Palestinian State

Israeli Settlement Blocs Annexed to Israel

Israeli Security Border

MEDITERRANEAN SEA

Jenin

Tulkarm

WEST BANK

Nablus

Qalqilya

Tel Aviv

While no map was presented during the final rounds at Camp David, this map illustrates the parameters of what President Clinton proposed and Arafat rejected: Palestinian control over 91% of the West Bank in contiguous territory and an Israeli security presence along 15% of the border with Jordan. This map actually understates the final Camp David proposal because it does not depict the additional territorial swap of 1% that was offered from Israeli territory.

Ramallah

Jericho

Maale Adumim

Jerusalem

ISRAEL

Jordan River

Bethlehem

Hebron

Dead Sea

0   10
miles

Copyright 2004 the Washington Institute for Near East Policy. Reprinted with permission.

Maps reflecting the actual Israeli proposal at Camp David (above) and the Palestinian characterization of the final proposal (facing page) at Camp David, July 2000.

Palestinian Characterization of the Final Proposal at Camp David

- Israeli Settlement Blocs
- Proposed Palestinian State
- Israeli Security Zone

MEDITERRANEAN SEA

Jenin

Tulkarm WEST BANK

Nablus

Qalqilya

Tel Aviv

This map reflects a map proposed by the Israelis early at Camp David, but it inaccurately depicts Israeli security zones carving the West Bank into three cantons, and includes Israeli settlements in the proposed Palestinian state. Official Palestinians now cite this map as the final offer they turned down at Camp David. (The initial Israeli proposal called for a Palestinian state in 87% of the West Bank. This map shows that state comprising only 83% of that territory.)

Ramallah

Jericho

Ma'ale Adumim

Jerusalem

ISRAEL

Bethlehem

Jordan River

Hebron

Dead Sea

0 ____ 10
miles

Map based on the
PLO Negotiations Affairs Department

Copyright 2004 the Washington Institute for Near East Policy. Reprinted with permission.

xiii

Map Reflecting Clinton Ideas

■ Proposed Palestinian State
□ Israeli Settlement Blocs Annexed to Israel

Haifa

Sea of Galilee

MEDITERRANEAN SEA

0 ——————— 15
miles

N

Jenin

Tulkarm

Nablus

Qalqilya

Jordan River

Tel Aviv •

WEST BANK

Ramallah

Jericho

Jerusalem • Maale Adumim

ISRAEL

Bethlehem

Gaza

Hebron

GAZA STRIP

Dead Sea

JORDAN

E G Y P T

No formal map was presented to the Israelis and Palestinians in December 2000 by President Clinton, but this map illustrates the Clinton ideas—a Palestinian state in 95% of the West Bank and 100% of Gaza. This map actually understates the Clinton ideas by not showing an additional 1 to 3% of territorial swaps to the Palestinian state from areas within Israel.

Copyright 2004 the Washington Institute for Near East Policy. Reprinted with permission.

Map reflecting Clinton's "parameters," December 2000.

Abbreviations

AHC	Arab Higher Committee
CO	Colonial Office (United Kingdom)
CZA	Central Zionist Archive
DFLP	Democratic Front for the Liberation of Palestine
DOP	Declaration of Principles
FO	Foreign Office (United Kingdom)
FRUS	*Foreign Relations of the United States*
HHA	Hashomer Hatza'ir Archive
IDF	Israel Defense Forces
ISA	Israel State Archive
IZL	Irgun Zvai Leumi (National Military Organization or "Irgun")
JNF	Jewish National Fund

LHI	Lohamei Herut Yisrael (Freedom Fighters of Israel or "Stern Gang")
NA	National Archives (United States)
PA or PNA	Palestinian Authority or Palestinian National Authority
PFLP	Popular Front for the Liberation of Palestine
PLO	Palestine Liberation Organization
PNC	Palestine National Council
PRO	Public Record Office (United Kingdom National Archives)
UN	United Nations
UNSCOP	United Nations Special Committee on Palestine

1 The Reemergence of One-Statism

Palestinian Arab Islamic fundamentalists, of the Hamas and Islamic Jihad varieties, have always advocated the elimination of Israel and a one-state—a Muslim Arab state—solution for the Israel/Palestine problem. But over the past few years, Palestinian Arab intellectuals linked to the mainstream Fatah Party and living in the West have also begun talking openly about the desirability, or at least the inevitability, of a one-state solution—one state between the Jordan River and the Mediterranean, inhabited by both Arabs and Jews. This marks a break from their at least superficial espousal during the 1990s of a two-state solution and a reversion to the openly enunciated policy of the Fatah and Palestinian Liberation Organization in the 1960s and 1970s, as embodied in the Palestinian National Covenant, which posited the elimination of the Jewish state and the establishment in its stead of an Arab-dominated polity encompassing the territory of Israel and the (at present) semioccupied West Bank and Gaza Strip.

For many of these "Western" Palestinians, this represents nothing more than an emergence from the closet. In fact, these current one-staters never really identified with the Fatah's professed advocacy in the 1990s of a two-state solution, with a partitioned Palestine divided into two states, one Jewish, the other Arab, living side by side in peaceful coexistence. Like their cousins in Palestine, both inside Israel and in the West Bank and Gaza Strip, and in the main concentrations of the Palestinian diaspora—Jordan, Lebanon, and Syria—they had always believed, and continue to believe, that all of Palestine belongs to them, the Palestinian Arabs; that a Jewish state in any part of Palestine is illegitimate and immoral; and that, in the fullness of time, the whole country will eventually revert to Arab sovereignty. But the Western—American and European—governmental two-state mantra and the PLO's apparent adoption of two-statism in the late 1980s and early 1990s forced them underground or into a duplicitous advocacy of, or reluctant acquiescence in, the two-state formula.

Now these Arab one-staters—the "all of Palestine is ours" advocates—are surfacing once again, loudly proclaiming the truth and justice of their cause. Ghada Karmi, a British Palestinian activist, perhaps heralded the trend with her article (albeit published in Arabic, in 2002) "A Secular Democratic State in Historic Palestine: An Idea Whose Time Has Come?" The question mark is misleading: the piece is quite emphatic about the unacceptability (to the Palestinians), indeed, death, of the two-state paradigm and the ineluctability of the one-state solution. She suggests that it might begin with "a formal policy of binationalism" that "may even ultimately pave the way to the secular democratic state in historic Palestine." (I shall return to the "secular democratic state" formula later.)

More significant still is Palestinian American historian Rashid Khalidi's admittedly cagey though ultimately unambiguous exposition of the one-state position in *The Iron Cage* (2006). He maintains in this book that his exposition does not "involve advocacy." But even a minimally perceptive reader will not miss where his heart and mind lie.

He writes: "Among some observers . . . a realization has been growing for years that this outcome [that is, a two-state solution] is increasingly unlikely. This realization has taken shape irrespective of the merits or demerits in principle of the two-state solution, in spite of the long-standing desire of majorities of Palestinians and Israelis for their own state, and notwithstanding the (often grudging and hedged) acceptance by each people of a state for the others . . . In this view, the inexorable cementing of Israel's hold over the occupied West Bank and East Jerusalem has rendered moot the possibility of establishing what could legitimately be called a Palestinian state [alongside Israel] . . . This is the case if a 'Palestinian state' is taken to mean a viable, contiguous, sovereign, independent state on the territory of the 22 percent of mandatory Palestine constituted by the Palestinian territories occupied by Israel in June 1967." This realization has "instigated renewed consideration of the old idea of a one-state solution, as either the ideal outcome or as the most likely default outcome, for Palestine/Israel." According to Khalidi, some see this one-state denouement as the "inevitable outcome of the extension into the immediate future of current trends . . . [These trends, amounting to] inexorable creeping de facto annexation [by Israel] of the West Bank and East Jerusalem, . . . will produce what is in effect a single sovereign Israeli-dominated polity throughout Palestine, with either rough Arab-Jewish demographic parity or, more likely, an eventual Arab majority. In this scenario, some feel, in time it will prove impossible to keep the two peoples in one tiny land segregated, or to keep that polity Jewish-dominated, as it eventually became impossible to keep South Africa white-dominated."[1]

Khalidi adds: "There is little reflection among those who hold this [one-state] conception about the future constitutional structure or political arrangements between the two peoples . . . Similarly, there is little consideration of how it would be possible in such a single state to overcome either the apparent desire of both peoples for independent statehood, or the deep and abiding distrust of each collectivity toward the other."

According to Khalidi, there is another group of one-staters whose thinking is a "throwback to the old Palestinian idea of a single unitary state of Palestine . . . [either] in terms of the previous PLO conception of a secular, democratic state in all of Palestine with equal rights for all . . . [or] in terms of an Islamic state in which non-Muslims would be tolerated minorities."

A last group of one-staters, according to Khalidi's definitions, are those who advocate "a binational approach . . . [that] would take into account . . . [the] two national realities within the framework of one state." Khalidi acknowledges that all the one-state approaches have not taken real account of the "stone wall" of Israeli and American rejection of the dismantling of the Jewish state and run counter to the international warrant of legitimacy for Jewish statehood (and Palestinian Arab statehood) issued by the UN General Assembly partition resolution (number 181) of November 1947.[2]

The precipitants to this newfound candor about the desirability, or at least the inevitability, of a single state between the Mediterranean Sea and the Jordan River (and often the assertion of "inevitability" is mere camouflage for the propagation of its "desirability") are three: PLO chairman Yasser Arafat's rejection of the two-state solution proposed in July and again in December 2000 by Israeli prime minister Ehud Barak and US president Bill Clinton, his rejection providing political impetus and cover for the in-principle subversion of two-statism; the rise of the openly rejectionist, one-statist Hamas to primacy in Palestinian Arab politics, as epitomized in the movement's general election victory of January 2006 and its violent takeover of the Gaza Strip in

June 2007; and, last, the recent advocacy of a one-state solution by a coterie of non-Arab Western intellectuals, spearheaded by Tony Judt, a distinguished professor of modern European history at New York University, against the backdrop of the Second Intifada and, more pertinently, the Islamic world's assault on the West, epitomized by 9/11 (and stretching, geographically, from the southern Philippines and southern Thailand through India, Afghanistan, and the Middle East to Madrid and London). I would like to focus for the moment on this third precipitant.

In 2003 Judt, who has never worked academically on the Middle East, published "Israel: The Alternative" in the *New York Review of Books*. This article can be seen at once as the harbinger and first blossom of this newborn one-statism among certain segments of the Western intelligentsia. For Palestinian one-staters, it was a public relations coup. It placed the one-state idea—or in Judt's view, "ideal"—buried, in effect, since the late 1940s, squarely and noisily on the table of international agendas.

Judt's arguments were fairly simple: the idea of Israel, as of ethnic nationalism in general, had (partly due to the Yugoslav wars of the 1990s) lost traction and was no longer adequate to underpin the continued existence of, and support for, a Jewish state. We are living "in an age" that rejects the idea of a state in which "one community—Jews—is set above others." The Jewish state, he argued, had been established "too late," "a characteristically late-nineteenth-century separatist project" superimposed on "a world that has moved on, a world of individual rights, open frontiers, and international law." Judt implied that, at least intellectually, the nation state was dead and "the very idea of a 'Jewish state' . . . rooted in another time and place . . . is an anachronism . . . [in] a world where nations and peoples increasingly intermingle and intermarry . . . ; where cultural and national impediments to communication have all but collapsed; where more and more of us have multiple elective identities . . . ; in such a world Israel is truly . . . [a] dysfunctional [anachronism]."

To this overarching, principled contention Judt added a second, of a more practical turn: the Israeli-Palestinian Oslo peace process of the 1990s, based on an assumed ultimate outcome of two states, had died, essentially because of Israeli obstructionism, and could not be resurrected. There could and would be no partition of Palestine/Israel into two states. And the demographic facts on the ground, given the Arabs' far greater birth rate, as well as the current demographic reality of Israel's Jewish population of 5.4 million and 1.3 million Arabs and the West Bank–Gaza Strip's combined population of 3–3.8 million Arabs—the exact number is in dispute—mean that Israel can not long remain both Jewish and democratic.

Within a decade or two, continued Judt, there would be more Arabs than Jews between the Jordan and the Mediterranean. (Indeed, Haifa University geographer Arnon Sofer has argued that by 2020 the total population between the Jordan River and the Mediterranean will reach 15.5 million, with only 6.4 million of them being Jews and most of the rest, 8.8 million, being Arab,

creating a binational reality, albeit with a substantial Arab majority.[3] The Palestinian Arab birthrate is the highest in the world.
The natural increase among Palestinian Muslims is estimated at
3 percent per annum; among Israel's Arab minority and the West
Bank Palestinian population, it stands at 3.1 percent; among
southern Israel's bedouin population it is 4.5–5 percent; and
among the Gaza Strip Arabs it stands at 3.5–4 percent per
annum. By comparison, in 2006 Egypt's annual population increase was about 2 percent, in Turkey 1.3 percent, and in Iran 1.2
percent. Israel's overall natural increase in 2007 stood at 1.5 percent.)[4] If Israel—the Jews—still ruled the whole of Palestine,
they would either have to throw out all or most of the Arabs to
assure the polity's Jewish majority and nature or institute an
apartheid regime of Jews lording it over a disenfranchised Arab
majority, something Israeli society would most likely abhor. Neither of these options, geared to maintaining the Jewishness of
the state, was realistic, argued Judt.

The only other alternative was for Israel to withdraw from the
territories and facilitate the emergence in the West Bank and
Gaza Strip of a Palestinian Arab state, which would allow Israel
to remain both (largely) Jewish and democratic. But this could
not and would not happen, said Judt; it is "too late for that."
There were "too many settlements [and] too many Jewish settlers." The 400,000 Israeli settlers implanted in the territories
since 1967 will not agree to live in a Palestinian Arab state, and
no Israeli leader will have the guts, or political power, to forcibly

uproot, abandon, or crush them, as David Ben-Gurion back in 1948 had crushed the dissident right-wing Jewish militias, the IZL (Irgun Zvai Leumi, or National Military Organization, which the British Mandate authorities called the "Irgun") and LHI (Lohamei Herut Yisrael, or Freedom Fighters of Israel, which the British Mandate authorities called the "Stern Gang"). The political, ideological, and economic trauma of such an uprooting, which could result in a Jewish civil war, would be too great for Israel to bear. Hence, it will not happen.

So what was the solution? According to Judt, it was "a single, integrated, binational state of Jews and Arabs, Israelis and Palestinians." And this, Judt rhetorically opined, was not just "increasingly likely" but also "actually a desirable outcome." After all, "most of the readers of this essay live in pluralist states which have long since become multiethnic and multicultural." He pointed to "London," "Paris," and "Geneva" as such pluralist milieus.

Judt, himself a Diaspora Jew, owned up that one of his motives in this advocacy was that "non-Israeli Jews feel themselves once again exposed to criticism and vulnerable to attack for things they didn't do [that is, Israel's behavior in the occupied territories]. But this time it is a Jewish state, not a Christian one, which is holding them hostage for its own actions." "The depressing truth," Judt told his readers, "is that Israel today is bad for the Jews."

The practicalities of turning Israel/Palestine into a binational state did not trouble Judt overmuch. It "would not be easy, though not quite as impossible as it sounds," he suggested. And the United States and the international community could help. An "international force" could guarantee "the security of Arabs and Jews alike," and anyway, "a legitimately constituted binational state would find it much easier policing militants of all kinds inside its borders."

Judt's article elicited a tidal wave of responses, most of them negative. An exception was Amos Eilon, an Israeli journalist and historian who recently decamped to a villa in Tuscany. He waded in with a few paragraphs of support ("Judt should be lauded," he wrote)—though he added, tellingly, that should a binational state with an Arab majority materialize, "the end result is more likely to resemble Zimbabwe than post-apartheid South Africa."

But most of the responses published by the *New York Review of Books* were extremely critical of Judt's piece, not to say thoroughly dismissive. Omer Bartov, a historian of Israeli origin at Brown University, wrote that the author was "strangely wrongheaded" and seemed to be writing from the perspective of "a café in Paris or London." Compared to which nation state was "Israel an anachronism"? Compared to Syria or Saudi Arabia or Iran? And if the comparison was to modern Europe, surely Poland and Serbia were equally anachronistic because they, too, are "based on a unity . . . of nation and state." Judt seemed to prefer, for Israel/Palestine, the model of interwar Poland, with its diverse populations, "rife with ethnic conflict and anti-Semitism." Or

Yugoslavia, "which [recently] broke up in a sea of blood." For Judt, these (unsuccessful) multiethnic models apparently were preferable to (peaceful) uniethnic nation-states.

In any event, according to Bartov, the binational model for Israel/Palestine is "absurd" because neither Israeli Jews nor Palestinian Arabs want it. Both groups seek to live in a country inhabited and governed by their own. On the Arab side, the Islamic fundamentalists regard shared sovereignty with the Jews as "anathema," and the moderates know that "a binational state . . . would spell civil war and bloodshed on an unprecedented scale." Two states, perhaps even separated by an ugly security fence, is a better idea by far, he concluded.

Michael Walzer, a political thinker at the Institute for Advanced Study in Princeton, took the ideological bull by the horns when he wrote: "Ridding the world of the nation-state is an interesting, if not a new, idea. But why start with Israel? Why not with France? . . . The French led the way into this parochial political structure that, in violation of all the tenets of advanced opinion, privileged a particular people, history, and language . . . Or [with] the Germans, or the Swedes, or the Bulgarians . . . all of whom have enjoyed these 'privileges' much longer than the Jews."

But "the real problem" with Judt's proposal, wrote Walzer, was that he was not really pointing the way to a binational state at all but "would simply replace one nation-state with another," for in "a decade or so" there would be more Arabs than Jews between the Jordan and Mediterranean, so what would emerge from Judt's "binational" polity would be another Arab nation-state. "This is the explicit goal of Palestinian nationalists, and the recent history of the movement hardly suggests that they have given it up."

Walzer wrote that Judt would have the citizens of his binational state rely on "international forces" for their security. But what people in their right mind would rely on such forces for their security? Rather, "the truth is that the Jews," or at least those who could, would rapidly depart from Judt's imaginary postnational state, which would resemble nothing more than "post-Habsburg Romania." (Judt had compared contemporary *Israel* to Romania.) Walzer added, bitingly: "I suspect that Romania would be an upscale reference."

One noteworthy response was published outside the *New York Review*, by Leon Wieseltier, in the pages of the *New Republic*. He wrote that Judt ("and his editors") had "crossed the line" from "criticism of Israel's policy to the criticism of Israel's existence"; the "alternative" in their title was not "for Israel" but "to Israel." Wieseltier pointed out that Judt failed to describe the character of his desired polity, which would quickly devolve into an Arab-majority state with a diminishing Jewish minority. It would be a terrorist state, not a democracy (look at the other Arab states, look at Gaza), in which an ethnic cleansing of the Jews would be more than likely. "Why is Greater Palestine preferable to Israel?" asked Wieseltier. "The moral calculus of Judt's proposal is baffling . . . Is the restoration of Jewish homelessness, and the vindication of Palestinian radicalism, and the intensification of inter-communal violence, really preferable to the creation of two states for two nations? Only if good people, thoughtful people, liberal people, do not keep their heads. But these are deranging days."

Judt's response to these criticisms was at once provocative and faltering. He kicked off by postulating that "the solution to the crisis in the Middle East lies in Washington. On this there is widespread agreement." (I would say that, on the contrary—and on this there really is "widespread agreement," at least among those who know something about the Middle East—the United States is completely powerless to effect a change in the rejectionist position of Hamas and the Islamic Jihad and the Palestinian majority that supports them, and it is only marginally influential with regard to Israeli policies on the basic issues. American [and European] aid cut-offs during the past two years have left no impression at all on the policy of the Islamic fundamentalists, and Israel's withdrawal from the Gaza Strip in summer 2005 had almost nothing to do with American pressure and almost everything to do with Ariel Sharon's character and calculations and Israeli self-interest.)

But this is to segue. After dismissing much of the criticism as "hysterical," Judt distanced himself, at least chronologically, from the binational postulate that was the core of his argumentation. Mankind, he agreed with Walzer, had not yet entered "a post-national, transcultural, globalized paradise in which the state has become redundant." "When I asked 'what if there were no place for a "*Jewish* state"?' I was posing a question, not 'imposing' . . . a binational alternative," he now argued. And he went on: "I wrote of binationalism . . . not [as] a solution for tomorrow . . . For the present . . . binationalism is . . . utopian." But peoples, he argued, change (look at Franco-German relations), as do their ideas of what is possible.

The Judt article, the telling ripostes notwithstanding, spawned a host of articles and books advocating the one-state solution. Clearly he had opened the floodgates, tapping into a strong current in the Arab world and in the Left and Right in the West that sought, simply, not Israel's reform or the reform of its policies, but its disappearance, however affected and however camouflaged. As to be expected, most of these publications were written by anti-Zionist, not to say anti-Semitic, Arabs and their Western supporters, though some professed to be doing this also for the sake of Israel's Jews.

Hailing "the taboo [that] has finally begun to fall"—as if to say that, in past decades, no one had ever questioned Israel's right to exist or lambasted the Jewish state—Daniel Lazar, a constitutional scholar and journalist, argued in the *Nation* in November 2003 that, contrary to Theodor Herzl's founding vision, Israel is beset by war; is, with "what little democracy it still has," "increasingly abnormal" among the democracies, which are steadily becoming multiethnic; is losing its Jewish population to emigration while Diaspora Jewry is flourishing; and is "one of the more dangerous places on earth in which to be Jewish" (apparently a reference to the actions and intentions of Hezbollah, Hamas, and Iran). And the world's "Jewish problem" has only been aggravated by Israel, as anti-Semitism burgeons in the Islamic world and, it would seem, in Europe and the United States as well wholly or partly in reaction to Israeli actions. Lazar favored a binational state "based on internationalism, secularism, and democracy." How exactly Palestine's Arabs would be persuaded to adopt "internationalism, secularism, and democracy"—for which they, like their brothers and sisters outside Palestine, are not famous—was not explained.

A far more sophisticated, thoughtful, and academic discourse, demonstrating that a one-state solution is increasingly inevitable given the continued expansion of Israeli settlements and the growing despair of Palestinians with regard to the progress being made toward a two-state denouement, was produced by Gary Sussman, of Tel Aviv University, in 2004. In "The Challenge to the Two-State Solution," he argued, looking at trends in recent Israeli and Palestinian thinking, that "the legitimacy, basis and support for separation between the two peoples are steadily being eroded, primarily by unilateral Israeli actions. Theoretically, this process can be reversed, but at present there does not appear to be an Israeli, Palestinian or international leader who can alter the trend . . . The bi-national state . . . will come about because separation is discredited and impossible."

Shortly before the appearance of Sussman's article, Omar Barghouti published a piece entitled "Relative Humanity: The Fundamental Obstacle to a One-State Solution in Historic Palestine." Barghouti, an independent Palestinian analyst and doctoral student, asserted that "the two-state solution . . . is really dead. Good riddance!" and that "we are witnessing the rapid demise of Zionism, and nothing can be done to save it." What remains is a one-state solution or, as he put it, "a secular democratic state between the Jordan and the Mediterranean, anchored in equal humanity and, accordingly, equal rights." But to this rosy outcome he quickly added a corollary: "the new Palestine" "first and foremost" must "facilitate the return of . . . all the Palestinian refugees."[5] Thus, at a stroke, he assured that the "binational" state he was proposing would instantly become a state with an overwhelming Arab majority.

Virginia Tilley, formerly of the Centre for Policy Studies in Johannesburg and currently a lecturer at Hobart and William Smith colleges, followed up the original Judt article with one of her own, "The One-State Solution," published in the *London Review of Books*. It kicked off with a motto by Edward Said: "The notion of an Egyptian state for the Egyptians, [and] a Jewish state for the Jews, simply flies in the face of reality. What we require is a rethinking of the present in terms of coexistence and porous borders." The rest of the article follows the selfsame logic. "The two-state solution . . . is an idea, and a possibility, whose time has passed." This is so because Israel's unrelenting settlement drive has made the unraveling of Palestine/Israel into two states impracticable—and "there can be no reversal of the settlement policy," much as the expulsion of the country's Arab population is unthinkable. So only a one-state solution, with Jews and Arabs coexisting, remains.

But Tilley admitted that for the Jews, "the obstacles" of converting their country into a binational entity were "clearly massive [and] . . . profound." Moreover, many Palestinian Arabs might have a problem with a "democratic secular state"—after all, "many now favor" an "ethno-religious state based on notions of Arab and/or Muslim indigeneity of the kind taking hold in Gaza" (a polite way of describing a totalitarian fundamentalist Islamic Arab polity). Still, a one-state solution it must be because of irreversible Jewish Israeli expansionist and racist actions. Israel's complete and successful pullout from the Gaza Strip in summer 2005, despite stiff opposition from Israel's settler movement—concretely and loudly demonstrating the settlement enterprise's reversibility—must have come as a rude shock to Tilley.

Tilley expanded substantially on these brushstrokes in *The One-State Solution: A Breakthrough for Peace in the Israeli-Palestinian Deadlock*, a 276-page tract calling for "real democracy, through a bridging of peoples and their histories. It has been done elsewhere against staggering odds [i.e., South Africa], and it can be done here." A one-state solution is possible and necessary. Again, it is the Israeli settlement grid, and the ideology and political forces behind it, that are the impediment to a peace based on a two-state solution. "No power," she wrote, "has the political capacity to effect any meaningful withdrawal" of the urban cores of the settlement enterprise. On its back cover, Judt defined Tilley's book as "of enormous importance," just as Tilley, inside her book, praised Judt for "breaking public U.S. political ground."[6]

Tilley's self-styled "breakthrough" one-state proposal was shortly to be followed by Ali Abunimah's self-styled "bold" one. The Palestinian American cocreator of the Electronic Intifada web site and, more recently, the Electronic Iraq and Electronic Lebanon web sites, Abunimah in 2006 published *One Country: A Bold Proposal to End the Israeli-Palestinian Impasse*. He, too, proposed a one-state settlement.

Giving history a series of mighty, distorting twists, Abunimah implied, ostensibly on the basis of his refugee grandparents' and parents' recollections, that there had been "peaceful coexistence between Jews and Arabs in Palestine before the creation of Israel"—and, if men and women of goodwill got together, this peaceful coexistence could be re-created.[7]

This recollected idyll is a whopper of truly gargantuan dimensions. Of course, on the individual plane, there were, here and there—in Jerusalem, in Haifa, perhaps in Jaffa—Arabs and Jews who interacted commercially and, in small numbers and on some level, even socially. But in general, British Mandate Palestine, between 1918 and 1948, was characterized by two separate societies that did not interact or live "together," except in the sense of sharing the same air and complaining about the same, or different, British officials.

And the truth is that since the fin de siècle, Palestine Arabs had been murdering Jews on a regular basis for ethnic or quasinationalist reasons. In 1920, 1921, 1929, and 1936–1939, Arab mobs had assaulted Jewish settlements and neighborhoods in a succession of ever-larger pogroms. Had the presence and actions of the occupying British army not contained them, such bouts of violence would no doubt have been more frequent, widespread, and lethal.

At one point Abunimah casually mentioned one problematic incident—the unprovoked murder by an "Arab mob" of sixty-seven defenseless Orthodox Jews in Hebron in 1929. But he then dismissed the implications by arguing that, ever since, Israelis have made too much of the matter and would do better to focus on the fact that "most of the city's [seven-hundred-strong] Jewish community were saved because Muslim neighbors protected them."[8] In fact, most were rescued by British police intervention and by the fact that many Jews successfully fended off their assailants for long hours—though, to be sure, Arab neighbors did save several families.

Like the previously quoted one-staters, Abunimah laid the blame for the evaporation of the two-state idea on the Israelis. Again, the settlement enterprise was to blame. "It is not credible that a society would invest billions of dollars in roads and housing that it truly intended to give up," he suggested.[9] Hence, Israel's advocacy of a two-state solution, as at Camp David in 2000, was never sincere; in reality the Israelis wanted, and want, all of Palestine for themselves.

So, only one idea remained: the one-state solution. More and more Israeli Jews, Palestinians, and Americans were recognizing this, argued Abunimah. Israel's "insistence on maintaining its exclusivist Jewish character, in spite of the reality that Palestine-Israel is and has always been a multicultural, multireligious country, is a chauvinistic appeal to ethnic tribalism that stands no chance in a contest against democratic and universalist principles," he concluded.[10]

Judt's article had the virtue of igniting debate about the possible parameters for a solution of the Israel/Palestine problem. And as some of his critics pointed out, these parameters have been on (and off) the table for many decades—indeed, almost from the beginning of the conflict and certainly since 1917, when the British assented to the creation of a Jewish "National Home" in Palestine, in the Balfour Declaration.

On one level, the debate is simply about Israel—whether it should or should not exist. This is both a moral and a practical question. The first, moral part, can be subdivided: Should a Jewish state have been established in the first place? And, once coming into existence, should it—now sixty years old and with some

5.4 million Jewish inhabitants—be dissolved or disestablished, at whatever cost that will entail (first to Israel's Jews and the Jewish people, and then to anyone else)?

With regard to the establishment of the state in 1947–1949, a prominent component in the moral equation inevitably will be at what cost this establishment was affected in terms of Palestinian Arab displacement and suffering. A subcomponent will also have to be: Who was to blame for this displacement and suffering, the Zionist movement and the Jews, the Palestinian Arabs themselves, or some combination of the two?

The moral questions, regarding both the rectitude of what happened in 1947–1949 and the proposed dissolution of the Jewish state in our time, are complex and ultimately insoluble; the "answers" inevitably will be subjective in the extreme. But the problem of Palestine/Israel and its solution, in present circumstances, is also a practical question. It is a political science question relating to the best possible ordering of human society or two human societies in a given space, taking account of demographics, geography, politics, economic realities, cultural matters, and so on. The question boils down to the best possible concatenation of demography and politics for the peoples living between the Jordan River and the Mediterranean.

In broad strokes, there are two possible futures for Israel/Palestine—as one state or, partitioned, as two states. There could also be a three-way partition, with Israel and two separate Palestinian states—one in the West Bank and another in the Gaza

Strip—but this division, based on the current political separation of the Hamas-run Gaza Strip and the Palestine National Authority–Fatah-run core of the West Bank, is unlikely to persevere because the Arab inhabitants of the two territories are one people, in every sense, and are unlikely for long to fly off in separate political trajectories. Furthermore, Gaza, given its minute dimensions (139 square miles, 25 miles from north to south and 4–7.5 miles from east to west), is hardly a candidate for separate political existence, though, of course, history is full of surprises. But it is unlikely that this will be one of them.

So it's one state, comprising the whole territory of British Mandate Palestine, between the Jordan and the Mediterranean (about 10,000 square miles), or two states, meaning the area of the pre-1967 State of Israel (about 8,000 square miles) for the Jews and the bulk of the West Bank and Gaza Strip (about 2,000 square miles) for the Arabs. There are a number of possible permutations. Let us first look at the variety of one-state solutions propounded in the past or present.

One possibility, which can be dismissed fairly rapidly, is that Israel/Palestine will be governed, as one political entity, by neither of its indigenous national groups but by a third party, from outside, be it the United Nations or a Great Power or a combination of Great Powers. The idea, given the apparent unbridgability of the basic political positions of the two sides, is not as outlandish as it seems. A number of countries were governed, as League of Nations mandates, by Great Powers between the two world wars. More recently, Germany, Japan, parts of the former Belgian Congo and former Portuguese/Indonesian East Timor were temporarily governed by great powers or the United Nations. Palestine itself was governed, between 1917–1918 and mid-1948, by Britain as a League of Nations mandated territory. Before that, Palestine was ruled by the Ottoman Empire, but this hardly applies, both because in the waning decades of the empire there was no substantial Jewish population in the country (in 1881 there were some 25,000 Jews and 450,000 Arabs, and in 1914, 60,000–85,000 Jews and 650,000 Arabs) and no real "national" conflict between Jews and Arabs, and because Palestine was not ruled as one political or administrative entity but as a collection of subdistricts, governed from the provincial capitals of Damascus or Beirut, or in the case of the Jerusalem subdistrict, directly from Istanbul. But the British Mandate proved unsuccessful, insofar as Whitehall failed either to find or to impose a solution for the Zionist-Arab divide or to prepare the population of the country for joint, unitary self-rule.

Given the growth of Palestinian Arab national consciousness and the Palestinian national movement since that time, as well as the realities of Zionist numbers and power, it is highly unlikely that either group would agree to the permanent suppression of its national aspirations within the framework of permanent international governance, and the violence that would almost instantly erupt, were such international rule to be imposed, would without doubt, sooner or later, undermine the willingness of any international administration to soldier on. Temporary international governance—conceivable though highly unlikely—would leave us where we were before, seeking a solution in the medium and long term to the Zionist-Arab conundrum. External, foreign rule over one political entity offers, it would seem, no solution.

More saliently, there are three realistic basic formulas for a one-state solution: a state with joint Arab-Jewish sovereignty, based on some form of power-sharing by the two ethnic collectives (à la Good Friday Agreement in Northern Ireland) or on individual rights without any collective ethnic entities and entitlements (à la postapartheid South Africa), both of which can be defined as forms of binationalism; a state ruled by Jews, with or without a large or small Arab minority; and a state ruled by Muslim Arabs, with or without a large or small Jewish minority. I write Muslim Arabs because the proportion of Christians among Palestine's Arabs has been declining steadily since 1947, when they were close to 10 percent of the population. Today less than 5 percent of Palestinian Arabs are Christians, and their numbers continue to diminish through emigration to the West (mainly from the West Bank—Bethlehem is now a Muslim-majority town). The proportion of Christians among Israel's Arab citizens is higher, but given far higher Muslim birthrates and a measure of Christian emigration, the proportion of Christians in Israel's Arab minority is also declining. So the Christian element in Israel/Palestine is negligible and politically irrelevant.

Palestinian Arab nationalists, of both the Fatah and Hamas

varieties, like to speak of Palestine's "Muslims and Christians" when selling their case in the West—but this is a propagandistic device, wholly lacking in substance and sincerity (after all, the main reason Christian Arabs have been leaving the Holy Land has been fear of the Muslims and of future Muslim excesses, which is also the cause of the emigration of Iraq's Christians). Many Christian Arabs from the 1920s through the 1940s would have been happy had British rule continued indefinitely, and some may have preferred Jewish to Muslim rule following the Mandate.

I will look at this more extensively later, but for now let me point out that the two simplest and most logical variants of a one-state solution are an Arab state without any troublesome Jews and a Jewish state without any troublesome Arabs. We are talking here about expulsion. The idea of an ethnically cleansed Palestine was raised consistently by the Palestinian Arab national movement from the 1920s through the 1940s, and there are good grounds to believe that that was the aim of the Arab onslaught on the Yishuv—the Jewish community in Palestine—in 1947–1948 (or, at least, that that would have been its outcome had the onslaught been successful). From the other side, the idea of a partial or full expulsion of Palestine's Arabs by the Jews was discussed and supported by much of the Zionist leadership in the late 1930s and the 1940s, against the backdrop of the Arab Revolt of 1936–1939 and the Holocaust, and in some way this thinking contributed to the creation of the Arab refugee problem in 1948.

So much, for the moment, for possible one-state solutions. Let us turn to two-state solutions. One two-state solution, harking back to the Jewish Agency–Transjordanian agreement of 1946–1947, would see a two-state partition of Palestine between the Jews and the Kingdom of Jordan, based on a Jewish-Israeli state in western Palestine and a Jordan–West Bank state—a "Greater Jordan"—ruled from Amman to its east.[11] Thus the partition—as also envisaged in the Israeli Allon Plan of the late 1960s—would see a two-state solution based on an Israeli-Jordanian division of the country, with no Palestinian Arab state and with most Palestinian Arabs living in the Jordanian-incorporated part of Palestine.

But, for the time being, such a two-state scenario, given the thrust and potency of Palestinian Arab nationalism, is highly unlikely, even though some Palestinian thinkers speak vaguely about a Palestinian-Jordanian federation or confederation to be established some years after a partition that sees a separate Palestine Arab state being established alongside Israel.

Most thinking, since 1937, about a two-state solution has revolved around the idea of a partition of the Land of Israel or historic Palestine between its two indigenous peoples, the Jews and the Palestine Arabs. Since the establishment of Israel in 1948–1949, and more emphatically since the late 1980s, thinking about partition has focused on the possibility of coexistence between a Jewish state, Israel, as territorially defined in the 1949 Israeli-Arab armistice agreements, and a Palestinian-Arab state to arise in the bulk of the West Bank and Gaza Strip.[12] Such a solution is espoused by the international community, spearheaded by Washington, and its achievement is the official policy of both the government of Israel and the PNA, headed by President Mahmoud Abbas (Abu Mazen). But whether such a settlement was or is desired by the Palestinian people and by Israel's Jewish population is another matter, as I shall discuss in the following chapters.

2 The History of One-State and Two-State Solutions

The Land

When looking at past attitudes toward possible one-state and two-state solutions to the Palestine/Israel problem, it is well to remember that there was a twenty-five- to fifty-year hiatus between the two groups, the Jews and the Palestine Arabs, in the emergence of modern national consciousness and the development of their national movements. This hiatus, or, rather, what underlay it—differences in mentality and levels of cultural, social, economic, and political development—was in part responsible for the difference in attitudes toward the evolving problem and its possible solution.

Political Zionism emerged in eastern Europe in the early 1880s, under the impact of the wave of pogroms unleashed by the assassination of Russian tsar Alexander II. By the late 1890s, the ideology and its proponents had given birth to a world-embracing, if relatively small, Zionist Organization. During the following decades the movement grew, and its message was adopted, or supported, by growing numbers until, by the end of World War II, most of world Jewry—that which remained after the Holocaust—much of Western public opinion, and most Western governments came to support the establishment of a Jewish state.

National consciousness began to develop among the Palestine Arab elite only in the early 1920s, shortly after it had taken root among the notables of Damascus, Baghdad, Cairo, and Beirut. Before the end of World War I, most Arabs in Palestine defined themselves as Ottoman subjects; as Arabs—meaning, they belonged to that large, amorphous Arabic-speaking collective, and territory, lying between the Persian Gulf and the Mediterranean, whose seventh-century origins lay in the Arabian Peninsula; as Muslims; as inhabitants of this or that village or town and members of this or that clan; and, vaguely, as inhabitants of "Syria," an Ottoman imperial province that traditionally included Palestine in its southwestern corner.

Only gradually thereafter did a national consciousness pervade Palestine Arab society and give rise to a mass movement. A Palestinian Arab national movement, with a popular base, can be said to have arisen only in British-ruled Palestine in the mid-1930s, against the backdrop of the Arab Revolt; and some would say, with considerable logic, that this occurred only a decade or more later.

The two movements emerged in completely different political environments and among radically dissimilar societies. Zionism emerged amid a social and intellectual climate of both burgeoning nationalisms and, in some ways, a countervailing ethos characterized by the rise of liberalism, democracy, socialism, and modernization. The Arab nationalist movements that arose on either side of World War I, including the distinct Palestinian Arab national movement, were born in largely agrarian societies dominated by Islam, with its exclusionist attitude to all religious "others" and resistance to change, by the narrow rule of political despotism, and by the tribal mores of autocratic clans and families.

Given these variant backgrounds, though both movements sought self-determination, they experienced asymmetric evolutions and political trajectories. And this affected their attitudes toward a possible solution of the emergent conflict over possession of the land. Put simply, the Palestinian Arab nationalist movement, from inception, and ever since, has consistently regarded Palestine as innately, completely, inalienably, and legitimately "Arab" and Muslim and has aspired to establish in it a sovereign state under its rule covering all of the country's territory.

The Zionist movement, while ideologically regarding the country as the ancient patrimony of the Jewish people and as wholly, legitimately, belonging to the Jews, has over the decades politically shifted gears, bowing to political and demographic diktats and realities, moving from an initial demand for Jewish sovereignty over the whole Land of Israel to agreeing to establish a Jewish state in only part of a partitioned Palestine, with the Arabs enjoying sovereignty over the rest.

Hence, the idea that Palestine, all of it, should become a unitary state—an idea shared by the two national movements during their emergence—dates back to the precipitous decline of the Ottoman Empire toward the end of the nineteenth century, when protonationalists and nationalists of various ilks began to sense that the empire was nearing its end and that its breakup was imminent.

But Palestine at the time was not ruled as a united, single, separate administrative entity. It was subdivided into districts, each ruled from a distant capital. The area of Palestine from the Ramallah-Jaffa line southward, to Gaza and Beersheba, was ruled directly from Constantinople, because of the area's political and religious sensitivity (Jerusalem and Bethlehem). The area to its south, down to the Gulf of 'Aqaba, was ruled from Damascus. The northern half of Palestine was subdivided into three *sanjak*s, or subdistricts, ruled until the 1880s from the provincial capital of Damascus and thereafter, until 1917–1918, from the provincial capital of Beirut. In both administrative arrangements, the two more northerly sanjaks, Acre and Beirut, each contained territory south of the Litani River that was part of the post–World War I British Palestine Mandate and the French Lebanon Mandate.

In other words, under the Ottomans the area traditionally known as "Palestine" (*eretz yisrael* in Hebrew or *falastin* in Arabic) was undefined administratively or politically, and its inhabitants, Muslim, Christian, and Jewish, rarely defined themselves as "Palestinians." (Arabs living in the pre-Crusader district encompassing southern and central Palestine, *jund falastin*, already from the eighth century sometimes referred to themselves, in a geographical sense, as *filastini*, or Palestinian. But they never used the term *filastini* as a political designation.)

Ottoman officials, Europeans, and modern Jews regarded the territory lying between the Jordan River and the Mediterranean Sea as "the Holy Land," on the basis of the early Jewish and Christian appreciation and designation of the land as such. Muslims subsequently adopted the term, although one thirteenth-century Arab text refers only to "the land around Jerusalem" (as far north as Nablus) as *al-ard al-muqaddasa* (the holy land) and the term *al-quds* (the holy) was used only for Jerusalem itself. As for Palestine, to many Muslims it was no more sacred than, say, Syria or Iraq or Egypt.[1]

The Jews, however, always regarded eretz yisrael or Palestine, whatever its exact geographical demarcation, not only as a political entity, imagined or real, but also as their holy land. Throughout their exile, which began in the first and second centuries CE, the Jews had regarded the country as a distinct territorial entity and, from the end of the nineteenth century, following the rise of political Zionism, as the separate, distinct goal of their political aspirations, which aimed at resurrecting Jewish sovereignty in that territory.

Arab nationalism, of which there had been some early but slight intimations in the decades preceding World War I, got into its stride only during the latter half of the war and in its immediate wake. A thin layer of the Palestine Arab elite began to consider "Palestine" as a separate geopolitical entity with a possibly distinct trajectory leading to self-determination and statehood during the 1920s, following the severance of Palestine from Syria through the French takeover of Lebanon (1918) and Syria (1920) and the British conquest of Palestine and Transjordan (1917–1918) and the subsequent institution during 1920–1922 of separate French and British mandates over these territories. From that point on, the Palestinian Arab elite struggled tooth and nail to deny the "Jewishness" of Palestine. (An exception was the leading Palestinian intellectual and politician Yusuf Diya al-Khalidi, who at the end of the nineteenth century wrote to Zadok Kahn, the chief rabbi of France: "Who can challenge the rights of the Jews in Palestine? Good Lord, historically it is really your country.")[2] An apt indication of this denial was provided by the Jerusalem Christian Arab educator Khalil al-Sakakini, when he fulminated in 1936 that the British Mandate's new radio station referred to the country in Hebrew as "eretz yisrael" (the Land of Israel). "If Palestine [*falastin*] is *eretz yisrael*, then we, the Arabs, are but passing strangers, and there is nothing for us to do but to emigrate," al-Sakakini jotted down in his diary.[3] This effacement of the "Jewishness" of Palestine has characterized the Palestinian Arab national movement ever since. The complete deletion of the Jewish presence in and history of the country is epitomized in the textbooks published by the Palestine National Authority since the 1990s, in the destruction by Palestinians of Jewish sites in the PNA-controlled territories during the Second Intifada (for example, the torching of "Joseph's Tomb" in Nablus), and in the repeated "historical" pronouncements on this matter by the leader of the Palestinian national movement between 1969 and 2004, PLO chairman Yasser Arafat.

The Jews

The Zionist movement—the expression of the Jewish national will for liberation from Gentile rule and for territorial self-determination—from the start envisioned Palestine, all of it, as the future venue for Jewish statehood. Indeed, by 1918–1919, the Zionist leaders were claiming a "Greater Palestine," encompassing both all the territory west of the River Jordan and a twenty-mile-deep strip of land to the east of Wadi 'Araba and the Jordan River, as well as the land around and south of the Litani River to the north (in present-day Lebanon), as the patrimony of the Jewish people, to be transformed, over time, into a Jewish state.

But given the geopolitical realities of the dying years of the Ottoman Empire, the movement was careful officially to avoid blunt expressions of its will to fully fledged self-determination, restricting itself to talk of a Jewish homeland or "homestead."

The latter expression—*Heimstätte*—was the term used by the First Zionist Congress, held in Basel, Switzerland, in 1897 and chaired by political Zionism's leader and prophet, Theodor Herzl, in its foundational resolution, defining the movement's goal. Interestingly, the congress, bringing together, for the first time, representatives of the various Zionist groups and societies that had sprung up in the 1880s and 1890s across Europe, but mainly in the tsarist domains, spoke of "the creation of a *Heimstätte* for the Jewish people *in* Palestine"—rather than of converting all of Palestine into the Jewish homestead.[4] The careful phraseology was the result of protracted debate among the members of the drafting committee. Talking bluntly about both all of Palestine and a sovereign state, it was felt, would antagonize the Turks and perhaps needlessly alienate Gentile supporters of Zionism.

But, to be sure, the movement's aim, from the start, was the conversion of the whole country into a Jewish state. That is how both Zionism's leaders and foot soldiers saw it. Vladimir Dubnow, one of the earliest settlers in Palestine, wrote to his brother, Shimon Dubnow, the historian, in October 1882: "The ultimate goal . . . is, in time, to take over the Land of Israel and to restore to the Jews the political independence they have been deprived of for these two thousand years . . . The Jews will yet arise and, arms in hand (if need be), declare that they are the masters of their ancient homeland."[5] A few months earlier, Eliezer Ben-Yehuda, another early settler, soon to emerge as the father of modern Hebrew, had written to a friend: "The thing we must do now is to become as strong as we can, to conquer the country, covertly, bit by bit . . . buy, buy, buy [the land from the Arabs]."[6] Both correspondents had meant the whole Land of Israel/Palestine. Immediately after the First Zionist Congress, Herzl had jotted down in his diary: "At Basle I founded the Jewish State."[7] He too had thought of nothing less than all of Palestine.

The early Zionists had been aware of the Arab presence in the country—there were just under half a million around 1882, the year the first Zionists came ashore in Jaffa. And there were, at the time, some twenty-five thousand Jews in the country. But the Zionists anticipated that with gradual or, perhaps, abrupt mass immigration, the Jews would eventually become the majority. As Ben-Yehuda put it in another letter, from 1882: "The goal is to revive our nation on its land . . . *if only we succeed in increasing our numbers here until we are the majority.*"[8]

The Zionists saw the Arabs as interlopers whose ancestors in the seventh century had conquered—or stolen (albeit from the Christian Byzantine Empire, not the Jews)—and then Islamized and Arabized Palestine, a land that belonged to someone else. And, in the nineteenth century, the vast majority of the Ottoman Empire's Arabs, though they shared a common language, historical consciousness, and culture, had no national ambitions or emotions; they were satisfied to live as subjects of the Muslim empire of the day. Negib Azoury, the former (Lebanese Christian) Ottoman official and herald of Arab nationalism, was both precocious and alone, in 1905, in foreseeing a clash between the nascent Arab nationalism (not nascent Palestinian Arab nationalism, which was nowhere then apparent, even in intimation) and Jewish nationalism. In *Le reveil de la nation arabe dans l'Asie turque*, published that year, he had pointed to "the awakening of the Arab nation and the latent effort of the Jews to reconstitute on a very large scale the ancient Kingdom of Israel." The two movements, he wrote, "are destined to fight each other continually until one of them wins."[9]

Zionist settlers began trickling into and settling Palestine in 1882. There may not yet have been Arab "nationalism," but the Arab inhabitants of Palestine quickly resented and feared the burgeoning Zionist influx as a threat to the "Arab-ness" of their country and, perhaps, down the road, to their very presence in the land. Starting in 1891 they began to petition Constantinople to halt the Zionist influx, land purchases, and settlement and, at first hesitantly and infrequently, began to attack Jewish settlers.

For their part, the early Zionist settlers did not see themselves as protagonists in a drama of contending nationalisms or as rivals for the land. Like European settlers elsewhere in the colonial world, they saw the natives as objects, as part of the scenery, or as bothersome brigands, certainly not as nationalist antagonists. And as Zionists, they took it as self-evident that the Land of Israel belonged to the Jews and to no one else.

The passing of the Ottoman Empire, the two-stage British conquest of Palestine in 1917–1918, and the promulgation, by

Whitehall, of the Balfour Declaration all reinforced Zionist ambitions to convert Palestine into a Jewish state. This was not quite what had been stipulated in the declaration, issued by the foreign secretary, Arthur James Balfour, on 2 November 1917. In it, the British had declared their support for the establishment of a "National Home" for the Jewish people "in Palestine." They had thus adopted the language of Basel. "National Home," to be sure, was a mite stronger than Heimstätte—but fell short of the idea of a full-fledged "state" (though, in expatiating on the declaration subsequently, Balfour, Prime Minister David Lloyd George, and other senior British politicians repeatedly spoke of a Jewish "state" as their intended, ultimate goal). The wording had deliberately left open the possibility that all of Palestine would become the Jewish "National Home" but also, alternatively, that the "National Home" would be constituted in only part of (a partitioned) Palestine.

The Zionist movement, while itself refraining from openly espousing the aim of "statehood"—indeed, officially the movement avoided using the "s" word down to the mid-1940s—continued, through the 1920s and the first half of the 1930s, wholeheartedly to cleave to the idea that all of Palestine would eventually come under Jewish rule.

In 1919 Chaim Weizmann, representing world Zionism, laid out the movement's claims before the World War I victors at Versailles. The map he presented, buttressing his oral presentation, spoke in effect of a "Greater Palestine"—all of Palestine west of the Jordan as well as the strip of territory just east of the river, to a depth of twenty miles (up to the Hijaz railway line), and the area of present-day southern Lebanon south of Lake Karaoun as constituting the requisite territory of the "National Home."[10]

This territorial configuration had first been set out in 1915 by Shmuel Tolkowsky, a Palestine Jewish citrus grower and researcher, and reworked in 1918 by Aaron Aaronsohn, the Palestine Jewish agronomist, and then adopted by the Zionist leadership.[11] Tolkowsky had been driven both by history and by the Jewish need for space in which to accommodate the millions of expected immigrants. The slightly different map by Aaronsohn was based on history and on hard economic-hydrological considerations. It related to—and literally and metaphorically was framed by—and incorporated in the prospective "National Home" the major regional water resources, including the Litani River basin, the sources of the Jordan River (which lie in large part in today's southern Lebanon—the Hasbani and Wazzani Rivers—and in the northern edge of the Golan Heights, the Banias Spring), and, to the south, the succession of east-west streams that feed the Jordan downstream (the Yarmuq, the Yaboq, and so on), in today's Kingdom of Jordan.

And, without doubt, in their maximalist territorial ambitions, the Zionist leaders, primarily Weizmann, were driven by the real or imagined biblical and historical images of the contours of the First and Second Temple Judean kingdoms, which under David,

Solomon, and Herod apparently also extended to the chain of mountains to the east of the Jordan, from north to south—that is, the Golan, the Gilead, Moab, and Edom.

The leadership decided, contrary to Tolkowsky's original proposal, to exclude the length of the Hijaz railway line from the Jewish National Home. The leaders recognized it as a "special Moslem interest," which serviced the Haj, but, persuaded by Aaronsohn, argued that economically and hydrologically, the hill country east of the river up to a line just west of the railway line should be joined to the core of Palestine west of the river.[12] In determining the northern borders, "the deciding factor is the question of water supplies," Weizmann wrote to Winston Churchill, the secretary of state for war.[13] The assumption was that this "Greater Palestine" would eventually have a Jewish majority through massive immigration from Europe.

Interestingly, these selfsame boundaries had been charted (though less precisely) in a book on Palestine's geography, published in April 1918, by none other than David Ben-Gurion, a rising star in Jewish Palestine's embryonic socialist politics, who was to succeed Weizmann as the foremost figure of the Zionist movement and as Israel's founding prime minister, and Yitzhak Ben-Zvi, a socialist who succeeded Weizmann as Israel's second president in 1952. The Ben-Gurion–Ben-Zvi borders were, in the west, "the Mediterranean Sea from Rafah . . . to the Litani River"; in the north, from the Litani River between Tyre and Sidon, eastward to the al-Uj River; in the south, a diagonal line

from Rafah to the Gulf of 'Aqaba and from 'Aqaba northeast-
ward to Ma'an; and in the east "the Syrian Desert," possibly
along longitude 37 narrowing to 36° 20′ as the line of demarcation moved southward to the Gulf of 'Aqaba. Eastern Palestine
thus included the Ottoman sanjaks of Horan and Kerak and part
of the sanjak of Damascus.[14]

Weizmann and Ben-Gurion had hoped, in the fluid post–
World War I circumstances, that Transjordan or at least the hilly
spine east of the Jordan would remain part of Palestine and open
to Jewish settlement, ultimately becoming part of the future
Jewish state. But in March 1921 Colonial Secretary Winston
Churchill met the Arabian Hashemite prince Abdullah and decided to deposit the area east of the river—henceforth dubbed
"Transjordan"—into his safekeeping, at least temporarily. The
official League of Nations Palestine Mandate of 1922–1923,
while nominally including Transjordan, specified that the area
east of the river would not be opened to Jewish settlement.
Henceforth, the British "High Commissioner for Palestine and
Transjordan," who sat in Jerusalem, in practice governed only
Palestine west of the river, with the area to the east ruled by Abdullah, under the supervision of a British "Resident" who an-
swered directly to Whitehall.

The mainstream Zionist leaders "gave up" Transjordan with
great reluctance. As Churchill was making up his mind on the
matter, Weizmann wrote him an impassioned, multilayered appeal: now that, through Anglo-French agreement, Palestine has

been "cut . . . off from access to the Litani, deprived . . . of the Upper Jordan and the Yarmuk and . . . the fertile plains [that is, the Golan Heights] east of the Tiberias [that is, the Sea of Galilee]," Britain should desist from denuding Palestine of Transjordan. Jewish settlement in the hills east of the Jordan would secure the area for the British Empire militarily. And "it should . . . be recognized that the fields of Gilead, Moab and Edom, with the rivers Arnon and Jabbok, to say nothing of the Yarmuk . . . are historically and geographically and economically linked to Palestine, and that it is upon these fields . . . that the success of the Jewish National Home must largely rest. Trans-Jordania has from earliest time been an integral and vital part of Palestine. There the [Hebrew] tribes of Reuben, Gad and Menashe first pitched their tents . . . Apart from the Neqeb in the south, western Palestine has no large stretches of unoccupied land where Jewish colonisation can take place on a large scale. The beautiful Trans-Jordanian plateaux . . . [lie] neglected and uninhabited . . . The climate of Trans-Jordania is invigorating; the soil is rich; irrigation would be easy; and the hills are covered with forests." And "the aspirations of Arab nationalism centre about Damascus and Baghdad and do not lie in Trans-Jordania."[15]

But Churchill was unmoved. And in the end, the mainstream Zionist leadership acquiesced in the victors' truncation of Palestine, formalized in Churchill's white paper of 1922. The 1918–1919 demand for a swath of land east of the river was dropped—

though periodically over the coming two decades, under the recurrent impress of Palestine Arab opposition to continued Jewish immigration and settlement, the Zionist leaders raised the possibility, among themselves and with Abdullah and the British, of opening up Transjordan, too, to Jewish settlement. But repeated British and Transjordanian rebuffs during the 1920s and 1930s eventually persuaded Ben-Gurion and his colleagues that looking east of the river for settlement venues was unrealistic, and they continued to focus their gaze and pin their hopes for the growth of the Zionist enterprise on the land lying west of the river and on the Negev Desert, down to the Gulf of 'Aqaba.

However, the right-wing fringe of the Zionist movement, which never won more than 20 percent of the votes in any major Zionist forum before 1948 (indeed, before 1973), stuck to the movement's 1919 map and goal of a pre-Churchillian "Greater Palestine." In 1925 right-wing journalist and defense activist Ze'ev Jabotinsky gave this vision political form by founding the Revisionist Movement in large measure to counter mainstream Zionism's acquiescence in the loss of Transjordan. The Revisionists denounced the Churchill white paper and demanded that Transjordan, all of it, be reintegrated fully in the Palestine Mandate, meaning that it become, or become again, officially, part of the promised "National Home." In April 1931, at the first world Congress in Danzig of Betar, the Revisionists' youth wing, the movement resolved "to turn the Land of Israel, on both banks of the Jordan, into a Jewish state, with a Jewish majority."[16]

Jabotinsky's vision included a large Arab minority in the Jewish state, with full individual civil rights but without collective "national" rights. That year, at the Seventeenth Zionist Congress, Jabotinsky spoke of resurrecting what he called the historic borders of the Land of Israel, on both banks of the Jordan.[17] He left vague his hopes and ambitions regarding the fate of the bulk of Transjordan, the area east of the Gilead-Moab-Edom line. But the Zionist majority rejected Jabotinsky's call—to which he responded by denouncing the congress and tearing up his delegate's card. He expressed his vision in the lyrics of a song, "The Left Bank of the Jordan," which included the refrain: "Two banks to the Jordan; one is ours—and so is the other."

BINATIONALISM

But if the Revisionists posited a maximalist territorial vision, extending eastward beyond the river, and the socialist and liberal mainstream of Zionism posited a Jewish polity encompassing only the whole area between the Mediterranean and the Jordan, there was also a cluster of minuscule groupings that advocated both "Zionism," in the sense of establishing a Jewish "center" and promoting at least substantial Jewish immigration to Palestine, and a state that was binational, whose identity would be equally Jewish and Arab and whose governance would be an Arab-Jewish condominium. The principal advocates during the Mandate period of a binational polity were Brit Shalom—literally, the peace covenant or the peace association—and its successor organization, Agudat Ihud (the unity association), and the Marxist Hashomer Hatza'ir Movement and, later, party.

Brit Shalom Brit Shalom was formally launched on 9 March 1926 by a group of Palestine Jewish intellectuals, most of them hailing from central Europe, clustered around Palestine's first university, the Hebrew University, which had begun operating in Jerusalem the previous year. Among them were Felix Rosenblueth (later Pinhas Rosen), a past head of the German branch of the Zionist Organization (later, an Israeli minister of justice); Shmuel Hugo Bergman, a philosophy professor; Jacob Thon, a prominent Palestine Zionist executive; and Yosef Sprinzak, a leader of the socialist Hapo'el Hatza'ir Party (later speaker of Israel's parliament, the Knesset).[18] Close to the group, though not members, were Judah Leib Magnes, the Hebrew University's founding chancellor and president, and Martin Buber, a prominent philosopher who immigrated to Palestine from Germany in 1938.

The initial spark for the founding of Brit Shalom seems to have been the realization, after a visit to Egypt, by Professor Joseph Horowitz, who founded the university's Middle East Institute, that Islam was on the rise and that Muslim scholars were deeply hostile to Zionism. He conveyed these thoughts to Arthur Ruppin, the prominent Zionist executive and sociologist, and other Zionist officials and Jewish scholars, at a meeting in Ruppin's home on 26 April 1925. Horowitz wanted "to persuade Jews and Arabs to work together," Ruppin recorded in his diary.[19]

By November Ruppin was speaking of a Jewish-Arab "under-standing under the watchword 'Palestine, a Binational State.'"[20]

That year, Ruppin told the Zionist Congress meeting in Vienna that "Palestine will be a state of two nations." Robert Weltsch, editor of the influential German *Jüdische Rundschau*, had predicted that the future of Palestine lay in the coexistence of the two peoples: "We do not want a Jewish state, but a binational Palestine community . . . We want to become once again Easterners," he wrote.[21]

Brit Shalom's aim, as defined in 1928, was to "pave the way for understanding between Hebrews and Arabs ['*ivrim ve'arvim*] for cooperative ways of living in the Land of Israel on the basis of complete equality in the political rights of two nations [each] enjoying wide autonomy and for various types of joint enterprise in the interest of the development of the country."[22] The group, consisting wholly of Jews, posited political parity between the two communities (despite the demographic asymmetry, at the time, of some 800,000 Arabs living alongside some 160,000 Jews). In 1930 Brit Shalom published a memorandum calling for "the constitution of the Palestine state . . . composed of two peoples, each free in the administration of their respective domestic affairs, but united in their common political interests, on the basis of complete equality."[23] A binational state was seen as the means to achieving this goal.

A split quickly developed within Brit Shalom regarding the core issue of Jewish immigration. The Arabs flatly opposed all

Jewish immigration. Some Brit Shalom stalwarts, like Akiba Ernst Simon, a Berlin-born educator and philosophy professor, were willing to make do with permanent Jewish minority status in the binational polity. In March 1930 Simon called on the Jewish Agency to restrict Jewish immigration and officially to declare "our desire to remain a minority" in Palestine (he usually spoke of a permanent "40 per cent").[24] Others, such as "Rabbi Binyamin" (the pen name of Yehoshua Radler-Feldmann), a journalist, and Ruppin, were less accommodating to the Arabs. Ruppin said: "What the Arabs are willing to give us is at most minority rights for the Jews in an Arab state, according to the pattern of minority rights in Eastern Europe. But we have already had sufficient experience of the situation in Eastern Europe [on this score]."[25]

In effect, Brit Shalom, which never had more than several dozen members, began to disintegrate in August 1929, against the backdrop of the widespread Arab riots, which claimed more than 130 Jewish lives. Among the dead were 67 ultra-Orthodox Jews slaughtered by an Arab mob in central Hebron. In the weeklong violence, the Arabs had persuasively demonstrated that they did not want the Jews in Palestine. In October, Ruppin recorded in his diary: "I have searched out my Browning revolver which has been lying in my writing desk undisturbed for ten years; now it lies on my bedside table. After all, one can never be sure that nothing will happen."[26]

During the following years, with the rise of a young, radicalized Arab elite and the start of massive Jewish immigration to Palestine from eastern and central Europe, Arab-Jewish relations in Palestine only deteriorated. Things came to a head in 1936, with the outbreak of the Arab Revolt, which sought to oust the British and suppress the Zionist enterprise. Ruppin despaired: "I have adopted the theory . . . that we are living in a sort of latent [permanent?] state of war with the Arabs."[27] Binationalism, he concluded, was nothing more than a pipe dream. Or as British Foreign Office official Alexander Cadogan put it, the dream of binationalism was "pure eyewash."[28] By mid-1936, for all effects and purposes, Brit Shalom had disappeared.

In 1939, shortly after the end of the revolt and on the eve of the outbreak of World War II, a group of former Brit Shalom activists along with Magnes began to contemplate a resurrection of the peace association. The new organization, Agudat Ihud, was founded in Jerusalem on 11 August 1942, with Magnes, Henrietta Szold, the director of the Youth Aliya Department of the Jewish Agency, Buber, Simon, and Moshe Smilansky, the head of the Farmers Association, on the presidium.[29] The association's platform included a call for Arab-Jewish cooperation and, while avoiding explicit reference to binationalism, called for "the creation in the country of a government based on equal political rights for its two peoples."[30] Magnes favored continued Jewish immigration (though not of dimensions that could either endanger the country's Arab majority or permanently assure the Jews' minority status. How a permanent, exact fifty-fifty parity could be assured he was never able to explain). He met repeatedly with Arab nationalist leaders. Yet his Arab interlocutors consistently opposed any Jewish immigration.[31]

Buber believed that the establishment of a Jewish state would lead to war for generations and would require the Jewish state to behave like a militarist nation, "and he does not want to be a citizen of such a state."[32] To say that Agudat Ihud—like Brit Shalom before it—had few supporters in the Yishuv would be a perverse understatement: ten months after its establishment, Agudat Ihud—which, unlike Brit Shalom, actively sought new members—had on its rolls only ninety-seven members (though its monthly, *Be'ayot Hayom* [Problems of the day], had three hundred subscribers and sold another three hundred copies in shops).[33]

Brit Shalom and Agudat Ihud also faced deep ideological co-nundrums. Translating the binational idea into a blueprint for political praxis proved immensely difficult. Some members were willing to commit to a permanent Jewish minority though they were unable to find a mechanism that would assure the minority's rights—indeed, safety—in an Arab-majority state. Others sought further Jewish immigration until numerical parity was achieved—though none knew how to assure its permanency or to practi-cally offset the Arabs' far higher birthrates. Still others—including, during World War II, Magnes—hoped that the Arabs would agree to open-ended Jewish immigration that would eventually result in a Jewish majority. All sought some form of political parity with the Arab community—through an equal number of Jewish and Arab autonomous zones and shared power in a joint government (whether or not there was demographic parity). But none knew how to finesse the problem posed to democratic principles by a Jewish minority enjoying equal powers with an Arab majority. Last, none knew how to persuade the Arabs, who wanted dominance in and over all of Palestine, to accept the binational principle.

Magnes Politically, the most important figure linked to Brit Shalom and Agudat Ihud was Magnes. He enjoyed a strong following among American Jews and was respected by the Mandate government; his diplomatic, oratorical, and intellectual skills also won the sneaking admiration of Ben-Gurion and other mainstream Zionists. The American-born and -trained Magnes, a rabbi and pacifist, viewed the call for a Jewish "National Home" in Palestine, to which he immigrated in 1922, as, above all, a call for the creation of "a Jewish spiritual, educational, moral and religious center," as he put it in a letter to Weizmann in 1913.[34] In this, he was an heir to the spiritual or cultural Zionism propagated by Ahad Ha'am (Asher Hirsch Ginsberg, 1856–1927), the great Russian Jewish essayist. Magnes supported immigration (or Jewish "ingathering" in Palestine) and hoped the country would become "the numerical center of the Jewish People."[35] He opposed the idea of conquest, which he called "the Joshua way," and did not believe in the Great Powers' right to dispose of the country as they saw fit.[36] Like the Jews, the Arabs also had historical rights to the country, he believed. So Palestine was the home of two peoples and three religions and belonged neither to the Arabs nor to the Jews nor to the Christians: "it belonged to all of them."[37]

The Balfour Declaration "contains the seed of resentment and future conflict. The Jewish people cannot suffer injustice to be done to others even as a compensation for injustice [over the centuries] done to them," he wrote in 1920.[38] The Jewish "National Home" should not be established "upon the bayonets of some Empire."[39] Magnes, like Buber, feared that the Jews in Palestine would "become devotees of brute force and militarism as were some of the later Hasmoneans, like the Edomite Herod."[40] Magnes dissented from Brit Shalom in that he believed that its desire for an accommodation with the Arabs was tactical and practical rather than deeply felt; he knew that most of its members, including Ruppin, who at times espoused the transfer of Arabs, were not pacifists.[41]

All of this left Magnes with a somewhat fuzzy picture of what a future Palestine should look like. He spoke variously about both open-ended "international control through a mandatory"— that is, perpetual rule by a foreign power—and "a binational [Jewish-Arab] government."[42]

The problem with binationalism, however—apart from mainstream Zionist opposition—was that Brit Shalom and Magnes could find no Arab partners, or even interlocutors, who shared the binational vision or hope. As Magnes succinctly put it as early as 1932: "Arabs will not sit on any committee with Jews . . . [Arab] teachers . . . teach children more and more Jew-hatred."[43] In this sense, things only got worse with the passage of time, the deepening of the Arabs' political consciousness, and the increase in Jewish immigration.

In 1937, in the privacy of his study, against the backdrop of the bloody Arab Revolt, Magnes took off the gloves: "The great drawback on the Arab side was the lack of moral courage. If only one man would step out now and brave his people and plead that his leaders should sit down with Jewish leaders, the situation would be saved . . . [but] not even one Arab stood up." Yet perhaps it wasn't so much a matter of the Arabs' lack of courage as of Arab convictions. "Islam seemed to be a religion of the sword," a momentarily despondent Magnes concluded.[44]

(Indeed, many observers defined the Arab Revolt as a jihad. After reviewing the testimony of Bishop Hajjat, the metropolitan of the Greek Catholic Church in Acre, Galilee, and Samaria, and other Christians before the Peel Commission, one of the commissioners concluded: "We were informed that though they [that is, the Christians] are not afraid of the educated Moslem or the Effendi class who live in the towns, they have come to realize that the zeal shown by the fellaheen in the late disturbances [that is, in 1936] was religious and fundamentally in the nature of a Holy War against a Christian Mandate and against Christian people as well as against the Jews."[45] Already in June 1936, two months into the revolt, the deputy inspector-general of the British Mandate police, J. S. Price, wrote, in summarizing the revolt, under the subheading "The Religious (Moslem) Aspect—Jehad or Holy War": "It has long been the considered opinion of students of the Palestine problem that real and prolonged disorder can only be stimulated and protracted through the medium of religion . . . There are now demands that Haj Amin al-Husseini . . . should declare a Holy War (Jehad). It is unlikely that he will do this openly as he is not prepared to stake his all . . . [But] there are . . . indications that this spirit is being engendered by the medium of the Ulamas (learned religious [figures]). Fullest prominence is likely to be given to any incident having a religious complexion . . . There are [already] allegations of defilement of the Quran."[46] He had a point. At the start of the revolt, the Palestinian Arab political parties established a supreme cabinetlike body, the Arab Higher Committee. Its founding declaration stated: "Because of the general feeling of danger that envelops this noble nation, there is need for solidarity and unity and a focus on strengthening the holy national jihad movement."[47] As the revolt unfolded, the mufti and kadi of Nablus toured the surrounding villages "preaching that anyone who killed a land seller would reside in paradise in the company of the righteous."[48] The language of the rebellious nationalists was commonly the language of jihad. ʿAbd al-Fatah Darwish, a penitent land seller, swore in May 1936: "I call on Allah, may He be exalted, to bear witness and swear . . . that I will be a loyal soldier in the service of the homeland. I call on Allah and the angels and the prophets and the knights of Palestinian nationalism to bear witness that if I violate this oath, I will kill myself."[49] A placard hung on walls in the village of Balad al-Sheikh, outside Haifa, after the murder of a collaborator, read: "Nimer the policeman was executed . . . as he betrayed his religion and his homeland . . . The supreme God revealed to those who preserve their religion and their homeland that he betrayed them, and they did to him what Muslim law commands. Because the supreme and holy God said: 'Fight the heretics and the hypocrites; their dwelling-place is hell.'"[50])

Magnes occasionally found an Arab willing to meet and talk with him—and ready to hear what he, Magnes, might be willing to concede. In 1936 he met Musa al-'Alami, a Palestinian Arab "moderate" and Mandate government senior official, and agreed to the limiting of Jewish immigration to thirty thousand per year. In late 1937 or early 1938, Magnes met the leading Iraqi politician Nuri Sa'id. Sa'id apparently proposed a ten-year truce during which the Jews would promise not to exceed 40 percent of the country's population (though Magnes later always insisted that he had never agreed to permanent minority status for the Jews).[51] But these contacts and their outcome were hardly the comprehensive, final binational accord Magnes was striving for. (And, of course, neither 'Alami nor Sa'id were leaders of the Palestinian national movement.)

By mid-World War II Magnes realized that an open-ended international mandate was no longer feasible. He had despaired of ever reaching substantive Jewish-Arab negotiations or agreement and decided that the only solution would be an externally imposed "union between the Jews and the Arabs within a binational Palestine." Further, he determined, this union would need to be subsumed or incorporated in a wider economic and political "union of Palestine, Transjordan, Syria and Lebanon" and linked to and guaranteed by an "Anglo-American union." And the binational state would have to be "imposed [on the Jews and Arabs] over their opposition" by the United States and Britain.[52] The binational state would need to be based on "parity," in terms of political power, between the two constituent groups, in order to guarantee the rights of whichever group was in the minority.[53]

By mid-1948, with the first Arab-Israeli war in full swing, Magnes was deeply pessimistic. He feared an Arab victory: "there are millions upon millions of Muslims in the world . . . They have time. The timelessness of the desert."[54] An Arab ambush on 13 April 1948 of a Jewish convoy bearing doctors and nurses traveling through East Jerusalem to the Hebrew University–Hadassah Medical School campus on Mount Scopus—in which seventy-eight were slaughtered—was in effect the final nail in the coffin of Magnes's binationalism. It was not that he publicly recanted. But he understood that it was a lost cause—and that his own standing in the Yishuv had been irreparably shattered. Within days, he left for the United States, and within months, never returning to Palestine/Israel, he was dead.

Hashomer Hatza'ir The Hashomer Hatza'ir Movement, founded in 1915 by Polish Jews in exile in Vienna, added a further element to the binational vision: socialism.

After World War I, Hashomer Hatza'ir groups immigrated to Palestine and set up a string of kibbutzim. In 1927, at the founding council of the movement's kibbutz association, Hakkibutz Ha'artzi, the leaders voted for a set of "ideological assumptions" delineating the movement's political "goal." Ratified as the movement's policy in the council's meeting in 1933, it stated (in the top-heavy Marxist terminology of the day): "In light of the maximal immigration of masses of Jews to [Palestine], which will create a concentration of most Jews in the Land of Israel and its environs [that is, hinting at Transjordan], and, on the other hand, [in light] of the fact of the presence of masses of Arab inhabitants in the country, the future societal development after the period of national liberation [from British imperial rule] by the socialist revolution and the cancellation of classes will lead to the creation of a binational socialist society."[55] Meir Ya'ari, one of the movement's leaders, put it in jargon-free Hebrew three years earlier: "Our aim is to realize a binational socialist society in Palestine."[56]

But the movement was still speaking of societal change, not statehood (to which, given its dormant anarchist tenets, it was vaguely antagonistic). World War II sped up the movement's transformation into a political party and pushed it toward greater political clarity. In 1942, at the sixth meeting of the Kibbutz Artzi council in Mishmar Ha'emeq, the movement at last spoke bluntly: "The political program of the Zionist Organisation should include the readiness to establish a political binational regime in the country, based on the unhindered advancement of the Zionist enterprise and governmental parity without taking account of the numerical ratio between the two peoples. Moreover, the Zionist Organisation should regard positively the perspective [that is, idea] of establishing a federative tie between the Land of Israel and the neighboring countries." The resolution called for continued Jewish immigration in line with the country's "maximal absorptive capacity"—and, during the transitional period before the Land of Israel fully integrated into the federation, "Jewish immigration would continue in dimensions that will assure that the Jews cease . . . to be a minority in the country." The binational state was to be based on "a common front and cooperative organisation between the workers of the two peoples"—in other words, a shared socialist outlook and goals. To this end Hashomer Hatza'ir would act to help "set up a socialist movement" among Palestine's Arabs.[57]

Apart from its Marxist discourse and socialist goals, Hashomer Hatza'ir differed from Brit Shalom in that it always sought to achieve a Jewish majority in the binational state (albeit with political parity between the communities, regardless of the demographic tilt). And, against the backdrop of World War II, it focused on saving European Jewry and solving Europe's "Jewish Problem."[58]

Other Advocacies of Binationalism Between the two world wars, for a time, binationalism also held attractions for mainstream Zionist leaders like Weizmann and Ben-Gurion. But their approach was always tactical. Given the reality of overwhelming Arab numbers, a binational model that gave Jews political parity, while allowing for continued Jewish immigration that they hoped would one day result in a Jewish majority, was ephemerally attractive, even though it ran contrary to the deepest Zionist endgame aspirations. Haim Arlosoroff, soon to be named head of the Jewish Agency's Political Department—and, as such, the movement's "foreign minister"—in 1922 asserted that there was no alternative to "setting up a common state in Palestine for Jews and Arabs as equal nations in their rights."[59] Eight years later, Weizmann wrote to a friend that "[for] now we should be content with a binational state."[60] Weizmann told the Zionist Congress, in Basel, in July 1931 that "the Arabs must be made to feel" that the Jews do not seek political domination—nor do they want to be dominated—and "we would welcome an agreement . . . on the basis of political parity."[61] Even Ben-Gurion, under the impact of the 1929 riots, briefly spoke of "absolute political equality" and "political parity." In 1939 he recalled that in 1930 he had been "in favor of political parity. I use this wording and not binationalism because the latter expression is not clear to me . . . In 1930 I tried to develop a complete constitution based on political parity in stages of development . . . Inside my movement I fought for parity . . . I went to the Arabs . . . [But] they did not want to hear about it ."[62] So far, he had said three years later, "not a single Arab leader has been found to agree to the principle of parity"—and this without even mentioning their complete and utter rejection of continued Jewish immigration.[63]

A variant of the binational idea that surfaced during the late 1920s and 1930s was the concept of cantonization or "regional autonomy." Each community would have a region or regions in which it ruled itself, with core powers relating to defense and foreign relations vested in a central authority, possibly located in Jerusalem. At least initially, the idea was that the British would continue to play this central governmental role—but some variants had it that the central government, either immediately or down the road, would be controlled by the majority population. At one point Mussolini was reported to favor the idea.[64]

Others did, too. The first British governor of Jerusalem, Ronald Storrs, in his memoirs, *Orientations*, published in 1937, wrote that cantonization, based on "two more or less self-governing communities or cantons, with certain matters reserved [for] . . . a [British?] High Commissioner . . . shines through the fog of mutual criticism and abuse as an attempt to deal constructively with a rarely difficult problem."[65]

But the idea appealed to neither side, as the Peel Commission insightfully pointed out that year: it contained "most, if not all, of the difficulties presented by Partition without Partition's supreme advantage—the possibility it offers of eventual peace." Cantonization, simply put, "does not settle the question of national self-government. Cantonal autonomy would not satisfy for a moment the demands of Arab nationalism . . . Nor would it give the Jews the full freedom they desire to build up their National Home . . . nor offer them the prospect of realizing on a small territorial scale all that Zionism means. And in the background, still clouding and disturbing the situation . . . [and] intensifying the antagonism between the races, would remain the old uncertainty as to the future destiny of Palestine."[66] In short, ruled Peel, cantonization would solve nothing.

TWO-STATISM

Peel Proposes Partition In effect, under the dual impress of resurgent violent anti-Semitism in Europe, spearheaded by Nazi Germany, and the Arab Revolt against British rule and the Zionist enterprise, the year 1936 marked a watershed. The first development underlined the urgent need for a safe haven for Europe's Jews, and as the Western democracies closed their doors to Jewish immigration, the Zionist leaders came to understand that it could be afforded only by a Jewish state. Hence the leadership's conclusion in the mid-1930s that it was imperative and urgent to establish a Jewish state and its readiness, running counter to the thrust of the previous fifty years of Zionist endeavor, to abandon the vision of self-determination in the whole Land of Israel. The mainstream leaders, after thorough and painful deliberations, concluded that to save European Jewry it was necessary to agree to partition and to accept a Jewish state in part of Palestine, and to push the possibility of a state on the whole Land of Israel out of their minds or at least to a distant, ill-defined point in the future. Only the immediate establishment of a Palestinian haven could save Europe's Jews.

The second development, the Arab Revolt, propelled the British to curtail Zionist immigration and to appease the rebels, in light of the British Empire's need for safe lines of communication, running through the Arab lands, which spanned the Suez Canal and the string of airfields running eastward from Palestine through Transjordan and Iraq. The British needed to pacify the Arab Middle East, which also harbored large reserves of oil, as they faced the prospect of a three-front global war against Japan, Italy, and Germany. The Zionists understood this and were keenly aware both of the open window of opportunity for Jewish statehood that was likely to disappear in short order and of the need to exploit it, immediately, even at the price of giving up a large part of Palestine.

These factors coalesced to push the Zionist leaders in 1936–1937 to agree to the principle of partition, as enunciated by the Peel Commission, sent out by the British in November 1936 to investigate the causes of the Arab Revolt and to suggest means of amelioration. The commission published its report in early July 1937. Magnes defined the report as "a great state paper . . . It is a pitiless document . . . It exhibits in all of its nakedness our miserable failure—the failure of each of us, Jew, Arab, English."[67] The commissioners recommended that the Mandate be dissolved and that something less than 20 percent of the country—the Galilee and the northern and central sectors of the Coastal Plain—be awarded for Jewish statehood, with the bulk of the rest (some 70–75 percent of the country) earmarked for Arab rule. The commission further recommended that the Arab area eventually be joined to Transjordan, to create a "Greater Transjordan," under the rule of the Hashemite prince Abdullah. (The remaining 5–10 percent of the country—Jerusalem and Bethlehem, with religious cachet, and a strip of land from these towns, through Ramla, leading to the Mediterranean coast—was set aside by the commission for continued British rule.)[68]

The Zionist movement spent July–August 1937 agonizing over the proposal. There were bitter debates within the leading parties, most notably the socialist Mapai, whose head, David Ben-Gurion, was the chairman of the Jewish Agency Executive (in effect, the Yishuv's "prime minister"), and then a full-scale showdown in the emergency Twentieth Zionist Congress, in Zurich. Browbeaten by Ben-Gurion and Weizmann, the congress, by a majority of approximately two to one, accepted the principle of partition while seeking to negotiate an enlargement of the prospective Jewish area, the less than 20 percent of Palestine being deemed extremely unfair and insufficient for the absorption of the persecuted millions who were projected to arrive.

But nothing came of the Peel proposals. They were rejected not only by the Palestinian Arab leadership and the Arabs outside Palestine but by the British government, which, after initially endorsing the recommendations, quickly about-faced. By May 1939, in the MacDonald white paper on Palestine, Whitehall completely disavowed the idea of partition and Jewish statehood and charted a future that, within ten years, would see the emergence of an independent Palestinian state governed by its majority Arab population.

The Peel recommendations had also provided for a transfer of a large part of the three hundred thousand Arabs who were living on the "wrong," Jewish side of the prospective partition line to the Arab-earmarked areas, or to neighboring Arab states, in order both to vitiate the possibility of irredentism and to provide space for the expected Jewish immigrants. One commission member, Reginald Coupland, in a "Note for Discussion" by the commission as it was preparing its report, compared the recommendation to the Greek-Turkish exchange of population in the 1920s: "Fortunately there is the encouraging precedent of the compulsory shifting . . . of 1,300,000 Greeks from Asia Minor to Thessaly and Macedonia and 400,000 Turks the other way round. The whole thing was done in 18 months, and since then the relations of Greece and Turkey have become friendlier than ever before. This is the ideal solution because it leaves no minorities to cause friction (as in Europe since Versailles) . . . The hardships of [the Greco-Turkish population exchange] . . . have been compensated by the creation of peace and amity."[69]

Ben-Gurion had used the Peel transfer recommendation to persuade the Zionist Congress to accept the offered ministate. And in private, he had added that he hoped that the emergent ministate would serve as a springboard for a future expansion of Jewish sovereignty over the whole of, or at least over additional parts of, the Land of Israel—indicating that his acceptance at that time of a partitioned Palestine, as a final settlement, was not completely sincere.[70]

Zionist Transfer Thinking and the One-State and Two-State Solutions
The Peel proposals opened the floodgates to Zionist discussion of the idea of transfer. The idea now had the imprimatur of the world's mightiest empire and oldest democracy, which also, it so happened, was charged by the international community with the fate of Palestine.

Not that Zionist thinkers and political leaders hadn't given the matter thought before. Indeed, while throughout the Zionist enterprise, since 1881, its leaders had looked to enhanced Jewish immigration as the primary means of achieving a Jewish majority in a land that, in the beginning, was 95 percent Arab, from the start some of them had toyed with the idea of speeding up the process through a transfer of Palestine Arabs to neighboring countries.

There is a glancing mention of the idea, albeit only once, in Herzl's diaries;[71] Ruppin, Leo Motzkin, Menahem Ussishkin,[72] and others occasionally proposed the notion; Frederick Kisch, chairman of the Jewish Agency Executive, in 1930, in a letter to Weizmann, recommended transferring Arabs to Iraq, which hungered, he believed, for additional manpower.[73] All thought in terms of a one-state solution covering all of Palestine and in which all or some of the troublesome, or potentially troublesome, Arabs, would be moved out to make way for Jewish immigrants and to speed up the process by which a Jewish majority would be achieved. A Jewish state with an Arab majority was generally regarded as inconceivable, and a Jewish state with even a very large Arab minority—say, a 55 to 45 percent ratio—was seen as highly problematic, not to say unviable. But although the transfer idea periodically gripped the imagination of this or that Zionist stalwart during 1882–1936, it was never adopted as a goal or policy platform by the Zionist movement or any of the main Zionist political parties, not then and not later. All understood that its adoption might alienate the successive Ottoman and British rulers of the land, and some, primarily socialists, also had moral misgivings.[74] At the time, though, the forced migration of populations usually did not exercise people's moral scruples. The Turkish-Greek exchange of population agreements, which involved massive, forced transfers of population in the 1920s, were in fact approved by the League of Nations and lauded by most Western observers. The prevailing view was that such transfers averted the persecution of minorities and the bloodletting engendered by majority oppression, minority rebellions, and communal clashes, not to mention irredentist wars, in which nation-states supported national or ethnic minorities living in neighboring states. This view was only reinforced during the 1930s when Nazi Germany used the German minorities question to subvert Czechoslovakia and Poland and justify the launching of what turned into World War II.

The transfer idea also impinged on, and was used to justify, the partition of Palestine and the two-state solution recommended by the Peel Commission and accepted by the Zionist movement. The commission had argued that for the two-state settlement to be viable, it had to be accompanied by a transfer of Arabs, or of "the Arabs"—"voluntary" if possible, "compulsory" if necessary—out of the territory earmarked for Jewish statehood. Otherwise, the emergent settlement would be plagued by irredentist upheavals and the Jewish state by a potential (Arab) fifth column, which would destabilize the settlement itself.[75] And Ben-Gurion used the Peel transfer recommendation to help sell the notion of partition—that is, of a two-state solution—to the many reluctant delegates who attended the Zionist Congress in Zurich. The Jews were getting only a small part of Palestine; it was therefore justified that, at the least, the area they receive be empty of Arabs. As he put it in a letter to his son, Amos: "We never wanted to dispossess the Arabs. But since England is giving [the larger] part of the country promised to us for an Arab state, it is only fair that the Arabs in our state be transferred to the Arab area."[76] At the Congress itself, Ben-Gurion had forthrightly declared: "We must look carefully at the question of . . . transfer . . . You are no doubt aware of the JNF's [past] activity in this respect [that is, in evicting Arab tenant farmers from land purchased by the Zionist institutions]. Now a transfer of a completely different scope will have to be carried out . . . Transfer . . . is what will make possible a comprehensive settlement program. Thankfully, the Arab people have vast, empty areas [to move to]."[77] A year later, expressing what was almost the consensual view of the Zionist leadership at the time, Ben-Gurion declared, in a closed forum: "With compulsory transfer we [would] have a vast area [for settlement] . . . I support compulsory transfer. I don't see anything immoral in it."[78]

Without doubt, the surge in Zionist leadership discourse during 1937–1941 about transfer was precipitated by the Peel recommendations. But even more important in its precipitation was what had engendered the Peel Commission in the first place— the Arab Revolt, which aimed at evicting the British from Palestine and rolling back, if not destroying, the Zionist enterprise. It was Arab attack, and the threat to Jewish existence in Palestine, that triggered Zionist transfer thinking, which aimed, in effect, to assure the Yishuv's continued existence and to reinforce it. Similar surges in Zionist interest in transfer had been registered in 1920–1921 and 1929–1930, immediately after previous bouts of Arab violence against the settlers.

Transfer thinking crested, if one is to judge by the protocols of internal Zionist leadership deliberations, during the years of the revolt and in the years immediately following under the impress of the Nazi persecution and then slaughter of Europe's Jews. With the Arabs threatening to slaughter Palestine's Jews and, through pressure on Britain, bringing about the closure of Palestine's gates to Jewish immigration, and with Hitler killing Europe's Jews and preventing them from escaping, the Zionists quite understandably sought the eviction of that Arab population which, by its actions, was indirectly contributing to the murder of their European kinfolk by helping to deny them a safe haven in Palestine and by threatening the lives of the Jews who already lived in the country. Hence, it is not surprising that Weizmann in 1941 spoke to the Soviet ambassador in London of the need to transfer half a million Arabs out of Palestine, as "a first instalment," to make room for two million Jews fleeing from Hitler's clutches in Europe.[79] And, moved by the selfsame logic that had motivated and persuaded the Peel Commission, the idea that partition and a two-state solution would have to be accompanied by a transfer of Arabs, or "the Arabs," out of the territory of the prospective Jewish state, was accepted during the countdown to the actual partition of Palestine, in 1947–1949, also by prominent Arab leaders, including Nuri Sa'id, Iraq's premier politician,

King Abdullah of Jordan, and Jordan's prime minister, Ibrahim Hashim.[80]

War eventually came to Palestine at the end of November 1947, and it lasted until 1949. It was initiated by the Palestinian Arabs and the Arab states, and they lost. The result was the country's effective partition, with Israel emerging with the lion's share (8,000 square miles) of the country, and the West Bank and Gaza Strip being taken over, respectively, by Transjordan and Egypt (together comprising just over 2,000 square miles). At the same time, the war witnessed a large-scale transfer of Arab inhabitants, with some 700,000 being displaced from their homes, about two-thirds of them coming to rest in other parts of Palestine (the West Bank and Gaza Strip) and one-third in neighboring Arab countries (primarily Lebanon, Transjordan, and Syria). Their flight and expulsion from the territory that became Israel was subsequently regarded by British and American officials as having solved the problem raised by the 1947 UN partition resolution, which had divided the country into a Jewish state on 6,000 square miles and an Arab state on about 4,000 square miles but had failed to address the prospective existence of a large, potentially disloyal Arab minority in the Jewish state-to-be.[81]

The War of 1948 had left in its wake a large—160,000-strong—Arab minority in Israel (which in early 1949 had some 700,000 Jews). That minority would increase, mainly by virtue of a high birthrate, to 1.3 million by 2007, when Israel's Jewish population numbered about 5.4 million (the Jewish increase overwhelmingly due to further mass immigration of Jews, primarily from the Arab world and the Soviet bloc). And the 1967 Israeli occupation of the West Bank and Gaza Strip added another 1.5 million Arabs to Israel's control, a number that had almost tripled, through natural increase, by 2007.

Hence, forever worried about demography and Jewish-Arab population ratios, some Israeli politicians continued to harbor, if not always publicly to speak about, the "transfer" idea. In 1949 and the early 1950s, generals like Moshe Dayan—later Israel's defense minister (1967–1974) and foreign minister (1977–1980)—and politicians like David Ben-Gurion, the prime minister in 1948–1953 and again in 1955–1963, thought occasionally about transferring Israeli Arabs to Arab states or Latin America and even initiated small, covert voluntary transfer (with compensation) schemes.

In the course of the 1967 War and in its immediate wake, some 200,000–250,000 West Bank and Gaza Arabs—many of them from 1948 refugee camps—moved to Jordan (Transjordan's new name). Nonetheless, some 1.5 million Arabs had been added to the area under Israel's control, again initiating a low-key debate in Israel about transfer. During the following years, a small pro-transfer political party, Kach, emerged, led by Meir Kahane; after it was outlawed (and Kahane was assassinated by an Arab gunman), a successor party was founded, Moledet, led by a former general, Rehav'am Ze'evi (who was also assassinated by Arab gunmen). Currently Avigdor Lieberman, a right-wing politician, heads the Yisrael Beiteinu Party, which supports the reduction of the size of Israel's Arab minority, either by agreed transfer or through the transfer to Palestinian sovereignty of slivers of Israeli border areas inhabited by Arabs (Umm al Fahm, Taibe, Kafr Qassam) in exchange for Palestinian agreement that Israel annex West Bank border areas inhabited by Jewish settler concentrations (Karnei Shomron, Elkana, Beitar Elit).

The idea of transfer—vis-à-vis Israel's Arab minority or the Arabs of the occupied territories or both—continues to characterize the pronouncements of some Jewish two-state advocates and one-staters. In both cases, reducing the number of Arabs or completely eliminating their presence is seen as facilitating the maintenance of Israel's Jewish character and grip on the territory under its control. But it is well to note that Kach and Moledet— single-issue transfer parties—at no time won more than 3 seats in Israel's 120-seat parliament, and Yisrael Beiteinu, which also represents other issues (such as Russian immigrant rights and benefits), is also a minority party (it won 11 seats in the 2006 general elections). And it is important to add that at various times over the past sixty years, especially during Arab assaults on Israel, particularly terrorist assault, many Israelis polled have supported the idea of transfer, their number ranging from 10 to 30 percent of the Jewish population. The thinking, or gut response, illuminating this posture is best conveyed in graffiti occasionally seen on walls of Israeli public buildings: "*No Arabs, no terrorism.*"

Two-Statism after Peel But to return to the theme of partition and two-statism: within the mainstream Zionist parties, the Peel Commission recommendations encountered strenuous opposition. People like Peretz Bernstein (of the center-right General Zionist Party) and Ussishkin, chairman of the Jewish National Fund, flatly opposed acceptance of the principle of partition. One-staters, they believed that a Jewish state without Jerusalem, Hebron, "[and] all the places that have been holy to us over the generations . . . is not a Jewish state, it is a political caricature . . . [and] a sin," as Ussishkin put it.[82]

But most of the opposition to partition within the Zionist mainstream—and the most significant debate was within the center and left, not between "Right" and "Left"—stemmed from pragmatic, political calculations rather than metaphysics and ideological considerations. One state simply made sense, geographically, politically, and economically. The problem, as Berl Katznelson, one of Mapai's leaders, put it, was that Zionist agreement to partition would merely truncate the homeland—but without resulting in Jewish-Arab peace; it would not lead to a settlement or to security for the Zionist enterprise.[83] Yitzhak Tabenkin, the ideologue of the socialist Ahdut Ha'Avodah Party, argued that the country was indivisible for practical geographic reasons and that a Greater Israel (*eretz yisrael hashleima*, the whole Land of Israel, or *ahiduta shel haaretz*, the country's unity) was necessary for reasons of immigrant absorption and settlement. But Tabenkin was also keenly attentive to the country's historical cachet, which drew Jews to Zion in the first place; without Hebron and Bethel and Jerusalem, the Jewish state would arise devoid of the magnetic loci of the historic homeland.[84]

On the right, Ze'ev Jabotinsky, the Revisionist leader, was consistently forthright. He rejected partition and spoke of a state encompassing the whole Land of Israel, which ultimately would have, he believed, a Jewish majority and a large Arab minority. It would be Jewish-ruled. He denounced the Zionist mainstream's acceptance of partition. "No Jew," he argued, could accept a Jewish state without "Jerusalem, Hebron, and the Land of Gilead [east of the Jordan]." It was a recipe for Arab irredentism that would continue to "covet" the Jewish area. Jabotinsky described the Peel proposal, positing a Jewish ministate, as providing "less than a drop in the ocean of Jewish distress, in the sea of its hunger for territory." He dismissed Ben-Gurion's secretly voiced hope that the ministate would serve as a "Jewish Piedmont," a springboard for future expansion (as Piedmont had served as the initial minuscule core of the Italian state during the Risorgimento). The Great Powers and the Arabs would not allow Jewish expansion, either through war or through "penetration" (that is, peaceful Jewish settlement in Arab areas).[85]

At the extreme edge of the Revisionist Movement in the 1930s stood the poet Uri Zvi Greenberg (*Atza"g*, in the Hebrew acronym), who preached the establishment of the Jewish state over the whole of the territory promised by God to Abraham and his seed, from the Euphrates in present-day Iraq to Egypt's Nile River. He even lambasted King Solomon and his heirs in the first millennium BCE for failing to achieve these borders and making do with the enlarged Land of Israel that encompassed the territory of Mandatory Palestine and a strip of land east of the Jordan.[86] Indeed, as late as 1950 he was writing, "When we reach the Euphrates, we shall sing a song of the nation."[87] A similar aim informed the writings of extreme right-wingers like Yisrael Eldad, a senior LHI figure from the pre-state days, who in 1960 wrote that "the Kingdom of Israel from the Euphrates to the Nile is not only possible, it is also necessary"; he called for the "liberation of the whole of the Land of Israel within the borders of the Divine promise."[88]

But Greenberg and Eldad represented only the wild fringe of the Israeli right—as Magnes, with his denunciation in July 1937 of the Peel recommendations, that even the establishment of a minuscule Jewish state "will lead to war with the Arabs," represented the fringe left.[89] In the solid center was the coalition of socialist and liberal parties led by Ben-Gurion. And whether or not Ben-Gurion in 1937 really resigned himself to partition and Jewish sovereignty over only part—a small part—of Palestine, during the following decade the Zionist mainstream, including Ben-Gurion, internalized and came to accept the principle of partition. The mainstream abandoned the goal of a Jewish one-state solution encompassing all of Palestine. To be sure, in no small measure it was the Holocaust that persuaded the Zionist leaders to make do with what history had to offer, while it was still on offer. But more important, between 1937 and 1947, the international community—under the impress of the Holocaust and the dictates of logic—had itself gradually come to accept the principle of partition and Jewish statehood in part of Palestine as the only reasonable basis for a solution to the conundrum. And the Zionist movement understood that it would have to bow to that community's will. History—meaning the British, the Americans, the Soviets, all under pressure by the Arab world and by the realities of Palestinian demography—would simply not award the Jews all of Palestine. So partition it had to be.

In 1946–1947 the Zionist leadership negotiated and concluded a somewhat hesitant, vague agreement on the partition of Palestine—a two-state solution—with Hashemite king Abdullah of Transjordan. In July 1946 Ben-Gurion drew up a partition scheme in which the Jews would create their state—"Judea"—in parts of Palestine and Transjordan and Abdullah's state—"Abdulliya"—would encompass most of Transjordan and the heavily Arab-populated part of Palestine (roughly the West Bank).[90] In principle, it was agreed between Jewish Agency representatives Elias Sasson (in August 1946) and Golda Myerson (Meir) (in November 1947) and Abdullah that a Jewish state would arise in the Jewish-populated areas of Palestine (exact borders were never discussed—but the Coastal Plain and the Jezreel and Jordan valleys were implied; the fate of Jerusalem was left open)—and that Jordan would occupy and annex the core Arab-populated area that included all or most of the territory subsequently known as the West Bank (Hebron, Ramallah, Nablus and Jenin, Qalqilya and Tulkarm); that Jordan and the Jewish state would live in peace; and, it was implied, that each would recognize and accept the other's sovereignty in the respective areas. The Jordanian takeover of the core Arab area of Palestine was approved by Whitehall in February 1948 as, implicitly, was the agreement with the Jews.[91]

But the wider international community had other ideas about the requisite two-state solution. The eleven-man United Nations Special Committee on Palestine (UNSCOP), authorized by the General Assembly and appointed by the UN Secretariat, examined the problem between May and August 1947 and on 1 September published its report. The seven-member majority (representing Sweden, Czechoslovakia, Guatemala, the Netherlands, Canada, Peru, and Uruguay) recommended the partition of Palestine into two states, one Jewish (with about 60 percent of the land), the other Palestinian Arab (with about 40 percent), with the Jerusalem-Bethlehem area being internationalized as a *corpus separatum*.

The Australian UNSCOP member abstained. But the three remaining members, representing India, Yugoslavia, and Iran—the first two with large Muslim minorities, the third, a Muslim country—submitted a minority report recommending a one-state solution, based on a "federal" state ultimately governed by the majority of its inhabitants, meaning the Muslim Arabs (Palestine at the time had some 600,000 Jews and 1.25 million Arabs, 90 percent of them Muslims).

The Zionist movement rejected the minority report out of hand (as did the West and the Soviet Union). Magnes, of course, saw in the minority report a "basis of discussion." He asserted that there were Arab interlocutors and potential partners—and even named one, Fawzi al-Husseini, who unfortunately had just been assassinated by his compatriots (see below): "This is the voice of an Arab brother, the authentic voice of our common Semitic tradition," he wrote, somewhat pathetically, to the *New York Times*.[92]

But not all Zionists welcomed the majority report (though, in Tel Aviv's streets, all Zionists, to be sure, danced for joy on the night of 29 November, after its passage, with some emendation, in the UN General Assembly). Already in 1946, Menachem Begin, head of the IZL —the Revisionists' military arm—denounced the prospective partition as "a crime," a "caricature, treason."[93] Reacting to the UN partition resolution, Begin denounced "the dissection of our homeland as illegal" and promised to continue the struggle to establish the Jewish state on both banks of the Jordan.[94] He was to speak in a similar vein on 15 May 1948, the day after Ben-Gurion declared Israel's establishment and hours after the Arab states invaded the country: a line drawn between "a nation and its homeland" is bound eventually to "disappear"; four-fifths of the homeland (that is, Transjordan) had been severed; Israel's "flag will yet be raised above David's Tower [in Jerusalem's Old City]" and "our plow will yet plow the fields of Gilead [east of the Jordan]," Begin declared.[95] He based his claim to both banks of the Jordan on the divine, biblical promise as well as on the history of the Jewish presence east of the Jordan in ancient times.

But these were minority views: the Yishuv's political mainstream full-throatedly hailed the UN partition resolution as a laudable turning point in Jewish history and endorsed a two-state solution. Ben-Gurion pronounced: "The UN decision to reestablish the sovereign state of the Jewish people in part of its future [sic] homeland is an endeavor of historical justice that at least partially atones for . . . what has been done to the Jewish people in our generation and previous generations."[96] This time, unlike in 1937, Ben-Gurion's declarations had the ring of sincerity, and he was to remain fixed in his advocacy of partition throughout the 1948 War while supporting the limited expansion of Israel at the expense of parts of the areas allotted to the Palestinian Arabs, on the peripheries of the core Arab area (Lydda, Ramla, and the Jerusalem Corridor) and in the northwestern Negev and southern Coastal Plain (Isdud/Ashdod and Majdal/ Ashqelon). It is true that on 26 September 1948 he tabled a motion supporting a renewed IDF offensive in parts of the West Bank (Ramallah and the Hebron Hills), which, if launched and successful, would have added East Jerusalem, and perhaps the whole of the West Bank, to the Jewish state; but he probably knew in advance that his fellow ministers would reject it, as they did in the vote that afternoon.[97] And later, in March 1949, just before the signing of the Israel-Jordan armistice agreement, when IDF general Yigal Allon proposed conquering the West Bank, Ben-Gurion turned him down flat.[98] Like most Israelis, Ben-Gurion had given up the dream of the whole land and had internalized the necessity, indeed inevitability, of partition and a two-state solution, be it because the Great Powers would not allow Israel to have it all or because of the unattractive prospect of coopting the more than half a million additional Arab inhabitants of the West Bank in the Jewish state.

Thus the 1948 War had ended in an effective two-state partition of Palestine, albeit between Israel and Jordan, and this settlement—based on the Israel-Jordan General Armistice Agreement of 3 April 1949—was essentially to remain unchallenged for two decades. While the Herut Party, the successor to the prewar Revisionist Movement, the Ahdut Ha'Avodah Party, representing the expansionist wing of the socialist movement, and a bevy of IDF generals longed, with greater or lesser ardor, through the years 1949–1967 to add the West Bank to Israel, the state, led by successive Mapai-dominated coalitions, preferred the territorial status quo and turned down every suggestion of an Israeli-initiated war with Jordan in pursuit of "Greater Israel." Even Ben-Gurion, who occasionally during the first post–1948

War years toyed with the idea of expansion, in the end always pulled back, his natural caution overcoming his ideological predispositions.

So the reality and necessity of partition—with the Jews retaining the eight thousand square miles of post-1948 Israel and the Arabs ruling the rest of Palestine (the two thousand square miles of the West Bank, with East Jerusalem, and the Gaza Strip)—held sway in the will and mind of the new state's political leadership. Given that Jordan had taken over the West Bank and that the area had not turned into the core of a Palestinian Arab state, the dominant Israeli view resembled the Peel partition scheme—which saw the core Arab area of Palestine ultimately joined to Jordan—rather than that of the UN partition resolution of November 1947, which had prescribed the emergence of a separate Palestine Arab state alongside Israel. But still, partition and two-statism governed Israeli political thinking and reality in those two decades before the Six-Day War in June 1967. The official policy of the successive Labor-led Israeli governments, under Ben-Gurion (1949–1953), Moshe Sharett (1953–1955), again Ben-Gurion (1955–1963), and then Levi Eshkol (from 1963), was to allow the territorial partition that resulted from the clash of arms in 1948 to stay. Indeed, no effort was made by Israel to exploit this or that local bout of hostilities to annex the West Bank or even the Gaza Strip (even though, in the wake of the 1956 Sinai-Suez War, when Israel conquered the Sinai

Peninsula and the Gaza Strip, Jerusalem made an unsuccessful diplomatic effort to block the Egyptian army's return to Gaza).

The Six-Day War—during 5–10 June 1967—temporarily undermined the Israeli majority's two-state outlook. In its brief war with Egypt, Jordan, and Syria, the IDF overran the West Bank, East Jerusalem, and the Gaza Strip (in addition to the Sinai Peninsula and the Golan Heights)—triggering powerful expansionist and messianic urges in the Israeli public, especially on the right and among religious nationalists.

Almost all Israeli Jews viewed the victory, which came immediately after weeks of despondency and genuine dread of a second Holocaust, as the Arab armies massed on Israel's borders, as miraculous and historic. It was a victory of the sons of light over the sons of darkness, who had threatened the Jews with destruction, and at the same time it marked a return to the central north-south spine of the Land of Israel—the historic heartland of the Jewish people and Judaism—that the IDF had failed to conquer in 1948. As Israel's defense minister, Moshe Dayan, put it at the time: "We have returned to the hill[s], to the cradle of our people's history, to the land of the patriarchs, the land of the Judges and the stronghold of the Kingdom of the House of David. We have returned to Hebron [the site of the tombs of the Patriarchs Abraham, Isaac, and Jacob, and their wives, and King David's first capital] and Shechem [where Abraham had erected an altar and where Joseph was buried], to Bethlehem [King David's birthplace] and Anatot [the birthplace of Jeremiah], to Jericho [the town conquered by the Israelite tribes as they entered Canaan under Joshua] and the fords of the Jordan at the city of Adam."[99] And the IDF had conquered East Jerusalem and, at its center, the Old City, David's (second) capital, the site of the First and Second Temples, and the capital of the Jews on and off from c. 1000 BCE until 70 CE.

The idea that the whole Land of Israel/Palestine, from the Jordan to the Mediterranean—for the first time in the modern era wholly under Israeli rule—should permanently remain under Jewish control, had received a major boost. Many religious Zionists regarded the victory as divinely ordained and as heralding the messianic redemption. And some secular Jews, moved by the grandeur of the moment, were driven to embrace the vision of "Greater Israel," meaning a policy geared to permanently holding onto the newly conquered territories for both historical-ideological and strategic reasons. Writers like Natan Alterman, Israel's leading poet, and Moshe Shamir, a major novelist—both men of the Left—signed on, as did a host of lesser figures, not only from the traditional Right but also from the center-socialist mainstream. Alterman called 1967 "the zenith of Jewish history."[100]

Even level-headed, moderate politicians, such as Prime Minister Eshkol, in those post–June 1967 days toyed at least briefly with the idea of permanently retaining the Arab-populated hills of "Judea and Samaria" (as the West Bank henceforward was officially called) and the flatland of Gaza. Dayan spoke of granting the Palestinian population "autonomy" and Eshkol defined the Arab inhabitants as "strangers"—resident in Palestine, to be sure, but usurpers of a land that was not theirs.[101] (But the retired elder statesman, Ben-Gurion, immediately— and iconoclastically—called for Israel to withdraw from the West Bank, though not from East Jerusalem.) And although on 19 June the Israeli cabinet secretly resolved to offer to hand back Sinai and the Golan Heights, respectively, to Egypt and Syria, in exchange for peace, it failed to agree on the future of the West Bank and Gaza.

The deadlock between "hawks" (who included Begin and, in this respect, Dayan), who for strategic or ideological-historical or religious reasons sought to retain these territories, and "doves" (including the powerful finance minister, Pinhas Sapir), who were willing to exchange them for peace, left the Israeli government paralyzed and in open-ended retention of these areas. And, to be sure, the Arab states did nothing to help. Indeed, having been humiliated in the war, the Arab League, at the Khartoum Summit in September, responded to the secret Israeli overture regarding Sinai and the Golan Heights—conveyed to Cairo and Damascus through the United States—with a resounding triple "no": "no" to recognition of Israel, "no" to negotiations, and "no" to peace.[102]

And by then, Eshkol, Dayan, and Yigal Allon, the minister of labor, had given the nod to hesitant settlement ventures, which included, at first, sites on the Golan Heights and in the 'Etzion Bloc area between Bethlehem and Hebron (the site of four kibbutzim razed by the Arabs in 1948).[103] Soon, the cabinet would also endorse Israeli settlement of, and around, East Jerusalem and in downtown Hebron. But at the same time, the Labor-led government pointedly refrained from supporting Israeli annexation of the West Bank or massive settlement of its Arab-populated hilly spine—though an expanded East Jerusalem was annexed within days of the end of the Six-Day War and the Jewish and Arab halves of the holy city were declared "unified."[104]

In July–August 1967, Allon, the veteran general from 1948 and now head of Ahdut Ha'Avodah, presented a plan that tried to square the circle—to hold onto (much of) the Land of Israel, Ahdut Ha'Avodah's traditional goal, while giving up the hilly spine, including Hebron, Bethlehem, Ramallah, Nablus, and Jenin; to expand Israel without adding Arabs. The plan called for the handover, in exchange for peace, of the hill country of the northern and southern segments of the West Bank to Jordan while retaining East Jerusalem and the almost unpopulated stretch of the southern Jordan Valley west of the river along with the whole western shoreline of the Dead Sea. The riverside was deemed crucial for long-term strategic reasons; the IDF must sit on the Jordan to prevent the entry of a large hostile army from the east (on the exgeneral's mind was principally Iraq, which had sent large expeditionary forces in 1948 and 1967). A narrow Jordanian-controlled east-west strip of land, running through the Jordan Valley at Jericho, would connect Jordan with the Arab core area of the West Bank. Allon was loath to hand over the core of the West Bank to the Palestinians lest, once under their rule, it serve as a springboard for future Palestinian irredentist pressure and campaigns to reconquer all of the country.

The Allon Plan harked back to the Peel Commission recommendations and the secret 1946–1947 understanding between the Jewish Agency and King Abdullah. It reendorsed a two-state solution—but with the Arabs receiving less of Palestine (only 70–90 percent of the West Bank) and with Jordan rather than the Palestinian Arabs as the political beneficiary. But there were two problems. First, no Arab ever accepted it as a basis for agreement, not King Hussein of Jordan (who wanted back all the West Bank, including East Jerusalem) or the Palestinians (the PLO wanted all of Palestine, and for the Palestinians, not Jordan); and second, it was unacceptable to the Israeli cabinet and, hence, never became official Israeli policy.

Allon could not swing a majority in the cabinet. So the plan both did and did not represent the policy and will of the Labor Alignment, the amalgam of social democratic parties in which Ahdut Ha'Avodah was in a minority, and the successive Labor-led coalition governments. Most Labor ministers vaguely supported the plan or some two-state variant. But the coalition cabinet, which always included parties of the Right—for a time, also Herut-Gahal and, throughout, National Religious Party representatives—refused to endorse it. Indeed, within weeks, the

Right declared, in the words of Menachem Begin, that it was "inconceivable" to "hand over to any form of Gentile rule . . . even one inch of our country"[105] (though after 1967 he was gradually and quietly to drop the Revisionists' traditional claim to part of Transjordan and to limit his vision of "Greater Israel" to historic Palestine west of the river).[106]

So the Allon Plan had a twilight life. It was the only game in town—and it wasn't; it was both on and off the table. Labor ministers repeatedly discussed it with Jordan's King Hussein, Abdullah's grandson. It appears that the Israelis initially offered Hussein some 70 percent of the West Bank—the hilly spine from Hebron through Ramallah to Jenin and the territory to the west, to the Qalqilya-Tulkarm line. Then, in the succession of secret meetings—with Eshkol's successor, Golda Meir, Allon himself, Defense Minister Moshe Dayan, Defense Minister Shimon Peres, and Prime Minister Yitzhak Rabin—they gradually upped the ante, according to Hussein, "to something like 90 per cent of the territory, 98 per cent even, excluding Jerusalem." But the king continued to demand all 100 percent, including East Jerusalem— "I could not compromise," Hussein recalled—and it was never completely clear whether he was offering full peace in exchange for the 100 percent (after all, he had signed on at the Khartoum Summit in September 1967 to the rejectionist "three nos").[107] So nothing was ever resolved or agreed.

In terms of the settlement enterprise, down to 1977 the Allon Plan more or less defined the contours of policy, meaning where settlements would be planted—in the Jordan Valley and the Judean Desert (along the Dead Sea), in the ʿEtzion Bloc and the Gaza Strip and Golan Heights—and where not. But the plan never served as the basis for a formal two-state proposal to the Arabs.

The Arabs

In the 1920s and subsequently, the Palestine Arabs defined Palestine, the country in which they lived and which they laid claim to, as the territory bordered by the Jordan River and the Mediterranean Sea and the area to the south, the Naqb (Negev) Desert, down to the Gulf of ʿAqaba, following the contours of the British Mandate borders. No clearly defined "*falastin*" having existed before, administratively or politically, they had no other definition to go by. (The pre-Crusader Arab province, *jund filastin*, with Ramla as its capital, had encompassed only part of the country. The north of Mandatory Palestine—the Galilee and the Jezreel, Beit Shean, and northern Jordan valleys—had been part of a separate province, *jund urdunn*, Jordan, whose capital was Tiberias.) Under the Ottomans, as mentioned, Palestine had been only a small part of a province, ruled from either Damascus or Beirut, and had been divided into a number of subdistricts, or sanjaks.

From inception, the Palestine Arab national movement, backed by the national movements and societies in the surrounding Arab countries, demanded that Palestine become an independent sovereign Arab state (except for the Syrian nationalists, who generally claimed and wanted Palestine as part of the future Syrian state) and rejected the notion of sharing the country with the Jews, either demographically, in a binational structure, or geographically, through partition.

The so-called Third Palestine Arab Congress, which can be seen as the conceptive venue of the Palestine Arab national movement, meeting in Haifa in mid-December 1920, called on the new British rulers to establish a government "to be chosen by the Arabic-speaking people who had lived in Palestine before the beginning of the [world] war." It completely, flatly rejected Jewish claims to Palestine: "Palestine is the holy land of the two Christian and Muslim worlds and . . . its destiny may not pass into other than Muslim and Christian hands." The Congress denounced the Balfour Declaration as contrary to "the laws of God and man."[108] (At the time, there were some eighty thousand Jews and seven hundred thousand Arabs in Palestine. About 10 percent of the Arab population was Christian. The Muslims were highly suspicious of their Christian neighbors. Many believed that the Christians were happy with British rule and favored its perpetuation. The reference in the congress's resolution to "Christian" rule is an obvious sop to the British—not an indication of a desire by the Muslims for power sharing with their Christian compatriots or of a concern for Christian interests.)

Henceforward, the Palestine Arab national movement continued to insist on a "national government" for Palestine and independence and to demand that Britain halt the "immigration of alien Jews, many of them of a Bolshevik revolutionary type."[109] The leaders of the national movement rejected the Jewish claims to the country and, indeed, the Jews' ties to the land: "We have shown over and over again," they wrote to Colonial Secretary Winston Churchill, "that the supposed historic connection of the Jews with Palestine rests upon very slender historic data. The historic rights of the Arabs are far stronger . . . Palestine had a native population before the Jews even went there and this population has persisted all down the ages and never assimilated with the Jewish tribes . . . Any religious sentiment which the Jews might cherish for Palestine is exceeded by Christian and Moslem sentiment for the country." The Jewish settlers were coming "to strangle" the local Arab population, and British policy would mean the Arabs' "extinction sooner or later," "the disappearance or subordination of the Arabic population, language and culture."[110] The Arabs wanted all of Palestine and refused to share power with the Jews or to divide the country with them.

THE ARABS AND BINATIONALISM

As Susan Hattis, the first historian of the binational idea in Palestine, has put it, the Arabs regarded the Jewish binationalists as "suspect, for as the Arabs saw them, they were simply a sugar coating on a bitter pill which the Arabs refused to swallow. The Arabs were usually suspicious of the Jewish bi-nationalists and their intentions, refusing to take them at face value." They viewed them as Zionists in sheep's clothing, ultimately pursuing and facilitating the emergence of a Jewish state.[111]

Even the most moderate-sounding Palestinian Arabs rejected binationalism. Sharing sovereignty with a people who were traditionally a subject minority, seen as alien upstarts and usurpers, and newly come, was unthinkable and contrary to every fiber of their Islamic, exclusivist being. But, given the reality of Mandatory rule and the necessity of attuning their arguments to Western mores, Palestine's Arab elite often, at least in public, brandished Western principles as the core of their argumentation. Hence, Palestinian spokesmen regularly invoked slogans like democracy, majority will, and one man, one vote—catchphrases and norms that, in fact, were completely alien to their history and social and political ethos and mindset. Thus the Jaffa-based Arab newspaper *Falastin* argued, in December 1929: "[We] support and will always support [anyone] . . . who is out for an honorable understanding and an equitable solution . . . which would inevitably lead to the establishment of the rights of the majority and the recognition of the rights and securities of the minorities."[112] But, following as they did the anti-Jewish pogroms of four months earlier, few Jews took such asseverations seriously.

Yet although Arab attitudes to binationalism were invariably dismissive, one variant, the cantonization scheme, earned at least passing, if tactical, approval from one important local intellectual. Ahmed Khalidi, the writer and principal of the Government Arab College in Jerusalem, thought that a settlement could be forged on the basis of Arab and Jewish cantons. He sent Judah Leib Magnes a memorandum, "Proposals for the Solution of the Arab-Jewish question of Palestine on the Basis of the Cantonization of the Country and the Formation of an Arab and Jewish state," dated 7 January 1934. The Arab canton, he wrote, should consist of the Gaza, Haifa, and Bisan areas and the present-day West Bank, with the Jewish canton consisting of the Tel Aviv–Atlit coastal area and the Jezreel Valley and Jordan Valley from Tiberias to the Galilee Panhandle (altogether on about 2.5 million dunams—or less than one-tenth of Palestine). He published his plan, anonymously, in *Falastin* on 27 December 1933. On 23 July 1934 he wrote Magnes: "I do not regard the Cantonization as an ideal solution, but perhaps it is as practicable as any other solution which has ever been proposed ... The move should come from your side ... It is understood that some transfer of property and population is bound to take place [and] ... two independent and widely autonomous local governments will be set up ... entirely run by Jews and Arabs with limited British advice." The country would remain for some time under British Mandatory rule. Jerusalem would be run by a Jewish-Arab-British council, which also would be responsible for "defense" throughout the country. Thereafter, the Arab canton would be joined to Transjordan, the whole under Prince Abdullah's rule. Each canton would have its own legislative council. Abdullah "will act as the head of the Executive Council of the two Cantons."[113]

In a follow-up letter, Khalidi told Magnes that "until the Jews realize that there must be some sort of reasonable limit to the practical application of the National Home both in land and population, it is difficult to see how the Arabs could be convinced to attempt to create a 'rapprochement.'" In other words, there needed to be a "reasonable fixed quota" on Jewish immigration, leaving "an Arab numerical majority versus a rich and enlightened Jewish minority." He added that "the friendship of the Arab should be in the long run more precious to Jews than obtaining millions of dunams or introducing thousands of [new] immigrants."[114]

In the end, Khalidi's plan envisaged a unitary state consisting of Transjordan and Palestine under Prince Abdullah's rule, with an autonomous Jewish canton in the Palestine lowlands and with a limitation on Jewish immigration, assuring a permanent Arab majority—not exactly the polity envisaged by the Jewish binationalists.

Musa al-'Alami, another Arab notable and a senior Mandate government official, at this time also supported a cantonization scheme, this time under overarching British rule. In his plan, the Jewish canton would be somewhat smaller than Khalidi's, limited to the stretch of coastline between Tel Aviv and Atlit. "The Jews may then bring any number of immigrants they like to that canton and may pass any legislation which they consider suits them best." The two cantons would be "under the guidance of the mandatory."[115] It is not clear whether he envisaged an end to British rule down the road or, if so, what system of governance would succeed the Mandate.

Such cantonization schemes continued to have at least a half-life in Arab circles, albeit as a means of bridging the hiatus between British rule and Arab sovereignty over all of Palestine. Norman Bentwich, the Mandate's attorney general and, from 1931, a Hebrew University law professor, reported after the publication of the Peel report that Jamal Husseini, one of the mufti's key aides, had told him that "both Jews and Arabs are in Palestine as of right . . . Both communities are opposed to a partition of their common home . . . The Arabs recognized the moral right of the Jews to a home in Palestine . . . it being understood that . . . Jewish immigration would, for a period of years . . . be limited by some relation to the existing population [ratios] . . . In the intermediate period, there should be autonomous government of Jews and Arabs, possibly on a cantonal basis."[116] Jamal Husseini, if he actually said these things, had been stunned by the Peel Report and seems to have momentarily grasped at canonization as a means of averting the implementation of the Peel recommendations, which included a full-fledged Jewish state.

(The cantonization idea would have one last effervescence—in the British-initiated Morrison-Grady Plan. In July 1946, Herbert Morrison, a British cabinet minister, and Henry Grady, an American diplomat, proposed a cantonization or "provincial autonomy scheme," with a small Jewish "province" along the Coastal Plain and a far larger Arab province in the central hill country, both enjoying autonomy in a federal arrangement under a British high commissioner for five years; Jerusalem and the

Negev were to remain under separate British control. There-after, the parties were to decide on a binational or a unitary state or partition. The Arabs flatly rejected the scheme, calling for im-mediate independence in all of Palestine; the Zionist leadership responded ambiguously.)[117]

In general, the Palestine Arabs opposed the idea of a bina-tional one-state entity in principle. In the early 1940s, one 'Omar Salah al-Barghouti, a member of the Opposition to Husseini, discussed the idea with members of the League for Arab-Jewish Rapprochement and Cooperation, a Jewish body led by Haim Margaliyot Kalvarisky, and with Magnes. The body, founded in 1939, included several ex–Brit Shalom intellectuals (Simon and Sali Hirsch) and representatives of the Marxist Left Po'alei Zion Party and Hashomer Hatza'ir in its ranks. Barghouti reportedly said that such a binational state could arise only within the framework of a pan-Arab federation of Middle Eastern states and appeared to agree to demographic parity at some point in the fu-ture between the Arab and Jewish populations. But he appears to have represented no significant element in the Palestinian Arab public or political opinion, and no agreement was ever signed.[118]

A few years later, a similar fate befell the more advanced nego-tiations between Fawzi Darwish al-Husseini, of al-Tur village, east of Jerusalem, and his minuscule Falastin al-Jadida (the new Palestine) group (as far as is known, there were only six "mem-bers") and the Rapprochement League—but this time a tragic twist was added. Al-Husseini, a participant in the Arab Revolt who had spent two years in British jails and the uncle of Jamal Husseini, was intrigued by Magnes's testimony before the Anglo-American Committee and his advocacy of binationalism, and sought to establish a joint Arab-Jewish political party or at least an Arab equivalent to the Rapprochement League. He sought "equality in everything . . . and the membership of a bi-national Palestine in a League of Arab States." On 11 November 1946 al-Husseini, in the name of Falastin al-Jadida, signed a vaguely worded agreement with the league. The agreement spoke of Arab-Jewish "cooperation," political equality, Jewish immigration limited only by the country's economic absorptive capacity, and the inclusion of Palestine in a league of neighboring Arab states. But twelve days later he was murdered by Arab gunmen. Simon concluded that "we are standing before a broken trough [meaning that an Arab-Jewish agreement based on binationalism was a nonstarter]." The Jewish Agency Political Department dismissed the episode completely, saying that Fawzi al-Husseini was a marginal figure, was fickle and had sold land to Jews (which may have been the reason for his murder), and was motivated by pecuniary considerations (the Rapprochement League had given him money to launch his political enterprise).[119]

Binationalism, indeed, had never found a toehold in any substantial segment of Palestinian Arab society. As Albert Hourani, one of the more reasonable al-Husseini spokesmen (he apparently loathed al-Husseini but, a wise man, kept his thoughts to himself), who went on to become a professor of Middle East history at Oxford University, put it in testimony before the Anglo-American Committee of Inquiry in 1946: "A bi-national state of the kind that Dr. Magnes suggests can only work if a certain spirit of cooperation and trust exists and if there is an underlying sense of unity to neutralize communal differences. But that spirit does not exist in Palestine ... If a bi-national state could be established—it would lead to one of two things: either to a complete deadlock involving perhaps the intervention of foreign powers, or else the domination of the whole life of the state by communal considerations."[120] There may still have been a few Palestinian Arabs, perhaps in Zionist pay, perhaps infused with vengeful anti-al-Husseini feelings (al-Husseini gunmen in the late 1930s and the 1940s killed a great many moderate Palestinians who had unforgiving fathers, children, and brothers), willing to join Magnes in his advocacy of binationalism. But they were largely silent and probably could have been counted on the fingers of two hands.

The thrust of Palestinian Arab nationalist feeling in the matter was officially laid out by al-Husseini's Arab Office—which represented the movement in Britain—in August 1947. Its memorandum (probably penned by Hourani), "The Future of Palestine," which was submitted to UNSCOP, stated:

> All responsible Arab organisations oppose binationalism uncompromisingly. The reason for this is clear. All these plans [that is, "political parity," "federation," and so on]

contravene the right of the majority to live under a government of their own choosing . . . Such plans are impracticable because a bi-national state of this sort cannot exist unless underlying the national differences there is a deep sense of common interest and common loyalty, which will determine the political action of both national groups in moments of crisis and in matters of importance . . . [Otherwise] each will watch the other with suspicion and growing hatred to see that it does not usurp more than its due; every question, however small, will be decided by communal considerations, and the gap between the two groups will grow ever wider. In these circumstances . . . either . . . life might degenerate from constant tension to civil war and its structure would dissolve into anarchy . . . [Or] foreign intervention might be sought and a foreign hand would always be required to hold the balance . . . The majority of the Zionists, there can be no question, desire the establishment of a Jewish state . . . The creation of a bi-national state would not satisfy them . . . [If there was a bi-national state, the Zionists would use it as a basis for efforts to dominate the Arabs] The fundamental Arab objection to the bi-national state is . . . one of principle: that to give a minority a political status equal to that of the majority is essentially undemocratic, the more so as it is certain that the minority will use its power to override the will of the majority . . . Furthermore, the condition put forward by the advocates of the bi-national state, that immigration should continue at least until the Jews reach numerical equality with the Arabs and possibly become a majority eventually, is again a denial of democracy, and if adopted would in fact turn the Arabs into a minority immediately. It is thus clear that the proposals for a bi-national state put forward by Dr. Magnes and his group are nothing but another way of reaching the objective of Zionism, that is, the creation of a Jewish state. For this reason, the Arabs regard the views of Dr. Magnes as no less extreme and perhaps more dangerous than those of the official Zionists, because they are cloaked in an aspect of moderation and reasonableness.[121]

THE ARABS AND PARTITION

If power sharing with the Jews within the framework of one state was out, there remained the possibility of coexistence, of two states, in a partitioned Palestine. But this, too, was anathema to the bulk of the Palestinian Arab leadership and, insofar as can be judged, to that of the Palestinian people, tutored by that leadership. Jamal Husseini's cousin, the mufti, Haj Amin al-Husseini, had bluntly told the Peel Commission that there could and would be no Jewish state in any part of Palestine.

Hence, there were few surprises in the Arab reactions, inside and outside Palestine, to the publication of the Peel Commission report in July 1937. Husseini and the AHC flatly rejected the

Peel recommendations, though, curiously, they did so in an initially hesitant fashion and only after eliciting the opinions of the neighboring Arab leaders. Most of these leaders were unequivocal. Saudi Arabia's king, Ibn Sa'ud, said that establishing a Jewish state was unthinkable in Islamic terms.[122] Iraq's prime minister, Hikmat Sulaiman, acting as the Arab states' point man, denounced the partition proposal and declared: "Any person venturing to agree to act as Head of such a [truncated Palestinian Arab] State would be regarded as an outcast throughout the Arab world, and would incur the wrath of Moslems all over the East. I declare both as head of an Arab Government and as a private citizen, that I should always oppose any individual ready to stab the Arab race in the heart."[123] Sulaiman's pronouncement was apparently backed by a fatwa by the Shi'ite ulema of Karbala and Najaf, who forbade acceptance of the "throne of Palestine" on pain of being declared apostate; "his evidence as a witness would be held inadmissible, he would be refused burial in a Muslim cemetery, and he would be held accursed until the day of Resurrection."[124] The potency of these Iraqi statements gained added weight from the fact that their barely veiled intended target, Emir Abdullah, a fellow Hashemite ruler, was Iraq's chief ally in inter-Arab politics.

And, indeed, Abdullah, a British ward, was the sole Arab ruler who (initially) spoke out favorably about the Peel recommendations, which had suggested that, eventually, the Arab part of Palestine would be joined to his emirate, under his rule. But within weeks he, too, fell into line with the rejectionist Arab position. In

September 1937, a gathering of politicians and other dignitaries from around the Arab world, meeting in Bludan, Syria, denounced the Peel proposals in unison.

The AHC declared that the proposals were "incompatible with [the] justice promised by the British Government" and called on the Arab states "in the name of Arab chivalry and their religious obligations to give support, advice, and assistance in order to rescue Palestine."[125] The Husseini position appears to have enjoyed widespread backing inside Palestine. A special correspondent of the London *Times*, after touring the country immediately after the publication of the Peel recommendations, reported: "Any Arab who makes a conciliatory move or does anything short of rejecting the partition scheme as impossible may expect to find himself denounced as a traitor or exposed to terrorism."[126]

So the stand of Husseini's internal Palestinian opponents, the Opposition, was not unpredictable. Through the 1920s and 1930s, the Opposition, led by the Nashashibi clan, headed by Ragheb Nashashibi, the mayor of Jerusalem (1920–1934), had challenged the dominance of the Palestine Arab national movement by the Husseinis and their allied clans. The Nashashibis had been sporadically supported by Emir Abdullah and the British, and, occasionally, Zionist officials were wont to call the Nashashibis, who in the mid-1930s launched the National Defense Party, "moderates" in counterpoint to the "extremist" Husseinis.

But the fact is that, although there was a difference in the tone of the two parties' pronouncements, in their methods (the Husseinis blithely used terrorism against both their enemies, the Jews and the British, and against their Arab rivals, primarily the Nashashibis) and in their seeming readiness to fall in with British plans, the two parties were at one in their objectives—a Palestine ruled solely by the Arabs, perhaps with a Jewish minority. Ragheb Nashashibi put it well in an interview with A. J. Brooks of the *Manchester Guardian:* "In fact, there is not among them [that is, the Palestine Arabs] any one Arab who can be described as 'extremist' and another as 'moderate,' for our cause is that of a whole nation, and our entire nation is in agreement . . . If those who use the words 'extremist' and 'moderate' believe that there are Arabs who could accept what the whole nation refuses [that is, partition], the only thing one can say about them is that their belief is without foundation."[127] Nashashibi apparently did not like being called a "moderate" (at least in Palestine and the Arab world). In fact, there were no substantive Arab "moderates"; there were spokesmen who sounded more mellow and mellifluous and others who sounded more radical. As one British senior official put it during the Arab Revolt (after the Nashashibis and Husseinis had become estranged), "All Arabs including Christians are quite definitely . . . utterly opposed to partition in any form . . . There is no moderate political opinion on this political issue."[128] The decades-long battle between the Nashashibis and Husseinis was over power and its benefits, not about a possible compromise with the Jews.

This explains in large measure why the Opposition, which on

3 July 1937 had left the AHC (for internal political reasons), supported the Husseini rejection of the Peel proposals published four days later. Perhaps to curry favor with the British and the Zionists, who provided the Nashashibis with funds, during the early months of 1937 the National Defense Party, against the backdrop of rumors that the Peel Commission might rule in favor of partition, appears to have expressed a measure of support for the idea.[129] And in the first days after the report's publication, Nashashibi informed the high commissioner of his backing for the Peel recommendations, or at least his acceptance of them "with reservations."[130] But on 11 July 1937, Ragheb Nashashibi declared flatly: "Palestine should be an independent Arab state without any Jewish or foreign rule,"[131] and on 21 July the National Defense Party sent a strongly worded rejection of partition to the high commissioner.[132]

Nashashibi was no two-stater or binationalist. He "fiercely opposed . . . Zionist ambitions," as his biographer, Nasser Eddin Nashashibi—no pro-Zionist himself—put it.[133] Indeed, as early as 1914, on the eve of elections to the Ottoman parliament, Ragheb Nashashibi declared: "If I am elected as a representative I shall devote my strength day and night to doing away with the scourge and threat of . . . Zionism."[134] But he was keenly aware of Palestinian Arab weakness and thought that "the only rational line to take is to be friendly and conciliatory with the British," that is, to try to wean them away from pro-Zionism and gain their support for the Palestinian Arab cause.[135] In short, Nashashibi's momentary support of partition, as of a series of earlier and later British proposals that in some way favored Zionism, was tactical.

His acceptance of Zionist help and his support for British efforts to crush the Arab Revolt in 1938–1939 must be seen in a similar light—though, to be sure, Nashashibi's efforts to establish antirebel "peace bands" that helped the British forces was regarded by the Husseinis as treasonable in the extreme.[136] Thereafter, the Husseinis spared no effort to kill off the "traitors" and "heretics" (the Husseini discourse throughout was as much religious as political; the revolt itself was dubbed a jihad). Fakhri al-Nashashibi, Ragheb's cousin, who had been instrumental in stirring up rural Palestinian disaffection with the rebels, was murdered in Baghdad by Husseini agents two years after the revolt. But the Nashashibis, while periodically supporting a Transjordanian takeover of Palestine, at no point, except for the momentary blip on the screen in July 1937, endorsed the establishment of a Jewish state.

A rejection of partition was also the emphatic stance of George Antonius in his *The Arab Awakening*, the classic, if lopsided, history of the rise of modern Arab nationalism, published in 1938. Antonius, a Christian Arab Jerusalemite, was among the moderate-sounding, Westernized Palestinian intellectuals. He lambasted, with some illogic, the Peel Commission partition and transfer recommendations by saying that they portended "eventual [Arab] dispossession" in, he implied, all of Palestine. "No room can be made in Palestine for a second nation except by dislodging or exterminating the nation in possession," wrote Antonius, framing the problem—as was the Arabs' wont—as a zero-sum game, in contradiction to the Peel approach of compromise by way of partition.[137] (Why Antonius believed, or at least argued, that partition with a transfer of all or some Arabs out of the less than the 20 percent of Palestine earmarked for Jewish statehood should result in Arab "dispossession" from all of Palestine is unclear.) Hence, for Antonius, the Arab fight from 1937 on, in the second stage of the revolt, was "essentially one of self-preservation . . . It is not possible to establish a Jewish state in Palestine without the dislodgement of a peasantry who seem readier to face death than give up their land."[138] Antonius added, titillating the conscience of Western liberals, that Jewish "distress" in Europe should not be solved at the expense of Palestine's Arabs—an argument that has been a refrain of Palestinian Arab nationalists ever since. "The treatment meted out to Jews in Germany and other European countries is a disgrace to its authors and to modern civilisation . . . [But] to place the brunt of the burden upon Arab Palestine is a miserable evasion of the duty [to absorb Jewish emigrants from Europe] that lies upon the whole civilised world. It is also morally outrageous . . . The cure for the eviction of Jews from Germany is not to be sought in the eviction of the Arabs from their homeland."[139] The "just" solution, according to Antonius, lay in constituting Palestine "into an independent Arab state in which as many Jews as the country can hold without prejudice to its political and economic freedom would live in peace, security, and dignity, and enjoy full rights of citizenship." The country's constitution would provide for "the protection of all minorities and minority rights . . . [and] enable the Jews to have a national home in the spiritual and cultural sense, in which Jewish values would flourish and the Jewish genius have the freest play." But, he added, Palestine was simply "too small to hold a larger increase of population."[140]

So much for further Jewish immigration. But, as well, Antonius left opaque his views regarding the disposition of the four hundred thousand Jews already resident in Palestine. The subject, even for a "moderate," necessarily required elisions, disingenuousness, and vagueness.

Such was the way of Westernized Palestinian Arab intellectuals. But this was not Haj Amin al-Husseini's way. As a rule, vagueness disappeared. The discourse of the Palestinian national movement's leader during the 1920s, 1930s, and 1940s was starkly expulsionist. Under his aegis, the Arab leadership sought and fought not only to halt Jewish immigration but also to roll back and destroy the Yishuv. Its mindset and ideology were expulsionist and, in great measure, anti-Semitic, though, given prevailing Western norms, they often obscured this in conversation with Europeans. But when speaking and writing in Arabic, they were nothing if not forthright. Husseini was later to write of the Jews: "One of the most prominent facets of the Jewish character is their exaggerated conceit and selfishness, rooted in their belief that they are the chosen people of God. There is no limit to their covetousness and they prevent others from enjoying the Good . . . They have no pity and are known for their hatred, rivalry and hardness, as Allah described them in the Koran."[141] Hence, it is unsurprising that the Arab mobs that periodically ran amok in Palestine's streets during the Mandate—in 1920, 1921, 1929, and 1936–1939—screamed "idhbah al yahud" (slaughter the Jews).

Occasionally, the leaders of the national movement, when pressed, let down their guard also with Western interlocutors. As early as 1919, spokesmen for the Jaffa Muslim-Christian Association, representing the Arab notability in Palestine's main town, told the King-Crane Commission, sent by the Allied powers to investigate the Palestine problem: "We will push the Zionists into the sea—or they will send us back into the desert."[142] Indeed, throughout the Mandate years the Palestinian Arabs viewed the conflict as a zero-sum game that allowed of no compromise and would necessarily end in one side's destruction or removal.

A noteworthy exchange occurred during Haj Amin al-Husseini's testimony before the Peel Commission in early 1937. The commissioners asked:

QUESTION: "Does his eminence think that this country can assimilate and digest the 400,000 Jews now in the country?"

AL-HUSSEINI: "No."

QUESTION: "Some of them would have to be removed
                   by a process kindly or painful as the case
                   may be?"

AL-HUSSEINI: "We must leave all this to the future."

On which the commissioners commented in their report: "We are not questioning the sincerity or the humanity of the Mufti's intentions . . . but we cannot forget what recently happened, despite treaty provisions and explicit assurances, to the Assyrian [Christian] minority in Iraq [the reference was to the massacre of more than three hundred Nestorian Christians by Iraqi troops at Sumayyil in northern Iraq on 11 August 1933. The massacre occurred despite government assurances of protection—which al-Husseini, when appearing before the commission, was not even bothering to offer the Jews]; nor can we forget that the hatred of the Arab politician [that is, al-Husseini] for the [Jewish] National Home has never been concealed and that it has now permeated the Arab population as a whole."[143]

Through the Mandate years, al-Husseini espoused a one-state solution in which only Jews who had been permanently resident in Palestine before 1917 (or, in some versions, 1914) would be allowed to stay (or, in another version, be granted citizenship). In 1938, one of al-Husseini's representatives, Musa Husseini, a relative, told Ben-Gurion that Haj Amin "insists on seven per cent [as the maximal percentage of Jews in the total population of Palestine], as it was at the end of the [First] World War."[144] In

September 1946 and January 1947, Husseini's representatives at the two-stage London Conference on Palestine repeated the formula that the Jews who had arrived in Palestine after 1917 were "invaders" and that the future Palestine Arab state would have to decide on their fate; the same position, which implied nonacceptance as citizens of those Jews who had arrived in the country after World War I (and perhaps a worse fate), was reiterated in the al-Husseini party newspaper, *Al-Wahda*, on 10 March 1947.[145] Husseini was to repeat a similar formula in 1974, shortly before his death in exile: "There is no room for peaceful coexistence with our enemies. The only solution is the liquidation of the foreign conquest in Palestine . . . and the establishment of a national Palestinian state on the basis of its Muslim and Christian inhabitants and its Jewish [inhabitants] who lived here before the British conquest and their descendants."[146] It is not without relevance that the Palestine National Council in the 1960s adopted a similar formula in the Palestinian National Charter (see below).

The fact that Haj Amin al-Husseini sat out most of World War II in Berlin, was employed by the German Foreign Ministry as a broadcaster of anti-Allied jihadist propaganda to the Arab world, and helped recruit Muslim soldiers in the Balkans to fight the Russians on the Eastern Front is clearly salient to understanding the thinking of the Yishuv during 1945–1948: Palestine's Jews believed that the Palestinians intended to slaughter them in a second Holocaust. And at least some Arabs, too, believed that such a denouement was imminent. Matiel Mughannam, the Lebanese-born Christian Arab head of the Arab Women's Organization, affiliated to al-Husseini and the Arab Higher Committee, at the start of 1948 told an interviewer: "[A Jewish state] has no chance to survive now that the 'Holy War' has been declared. All the Jews will eventually be massacred."[147]

Nor was this expulsionist, or eliminationist, mindset restricted to the Palestinian Arab leadership; some Arab states' leaders also occasionally gave it free rein. At the end of 1947 King Ibn Sa'ud wrote to US president Harry Truman: "The Arabs have definitely decided to oppose [the] establishment of a Jewish state . . . Even if it is supposed that the Jews will succeed in gaining support . . . by their oppressive and tyrannous means and their money, such a state must perish in a short time. The Arab will isolate such a state from the world and will lay siege until it dies by famine . . . Its end will be the same as that of [the] Crusader states."[148]

THE 1960S

The 1948 War had ended with Palestine in the hands of Israel, Jordan (the West Bank), and Egypt (the Gaza Strip), with no Palestinian Arab state. Arab society in Palestine had been shattered. About 60 percent of Palestinians had been displaced from their homes and were living in orchards, empty buildings, and newly established refugee camps, largely in the West Bank and Gaza, with the remainder in Lebanon, Syria, and Transjordan. The Palestinian political and military elite had dispersed to the seven winds, and Palestinian political institutions had disappeared.

During the 1950s, there was a measure of organized cross-border guerrilla and terrorist raiding by Palestinians against Israel, some of it orchestrated by Egyptian military intelligence. But it didn't amount to much, and Palestinian politics were dead. Things began to change in the early 1960s, when a handful of nationalist and pan-Arab Palestinians began to organize in the lands of their dispersion the rudiments of a resistance movement. In 1964, Egypt, partly for internal Arab reasons, arranged the convocation of a Palestine National Council, consisting of representatives of the Palestinian communities and organizations in Palestine and the Palestinian diaspora. The PNC first met in Jerusalem in May 1964, there establishing an executive wing, the Palestine Liberation Organization, with a former al-Husseini aide, Ahmed Shukeiry, as its first president.

At that meeting, the PNC set out its political goals in a document entitled "The Palestinian National Charter (or Covenant)," henceforward the PLO's constitution. In it, the "forces of international Zionism" are defined as "evil" and the Palestinian people are enjoined "to move forward on the path of holy war [jihad] until complete and final victory."

Zionism is defined as "a colonialist movement, aggressive and expansionist in its goal, racist in its configuration, and fascist in its means and aims . . . Zionism [is] an illegal movement and [the nations should] outlaw its presence and activities." Palestine is "an Arab homeland . . . [and] part of the great Arab homeland." "Palestine, with its boundaries at the time of the British Mandate, is an indivisible territorial unit . . . The people of Palestine [will] determine its destiny when it completes the liberation of its homeland." "The people of Palestine" are defined as "those Arab citizens who were living normally in Palestine up to 1947, whether they remained or were expelled. [Moreover], every child who was born to a Palestinian father after this date, whether in Palestine or outside, is a Palestinian." The charter goes on to declare: "Jews of Palestine origin are considered Palestinians if they are willing to live peacefully and loyally in Palestine . . . The partitioning of Palestine, which took place in 1947, and the establishment of Israel are illegal and null and void . . . The Balfour Declaration . . . [is] null and void. The claims of historic and spiritual ties between Jews and Palestine are not in agreement with the facts of history or with the true basis of sound statehood. Judaism, because it is a divine religion, is not a nationality with independent existence. Furthermore, the Jews are not one people with an independent personality because they are citizens in their [various] states."

Article 15 states that the liberation of Palestine will lead to peace and that the "Holy Places will be safeguarded, and the freedom of worship and to visit will be guaranteed for all, without any discrimination of race, color, language, or religion."

During the following three years the PLO's constituent organizations, led by Fatah (see below), with Syrian assistance, oc-

casionally raided Israel, to no great effect. But the Middle Eastern strategic picture changed dramatically with Israel's victory in
the Six-Day War in June 1967. The Palestinian organizations
were both thrown into disarray and revitalized; the Arab states'
defeat—with their armies hors de combat—seemingly thrust the
organizations into the forefront of the struggle against Israel.
There was a resurgence of Palestinian guerrilla and terrorist attacks in the newly occupied West Bank and Gaza Strip and in Israel proper. There was also a substantive emendation of the
Palestinian National Charter. At its meeting of 1–17 July 1968,
the PNC removed a number of loopholes in the original document and clarified various clauses. Article 15 now stated: "The
liberation of Palestine . . . is a national duty . . . and aims at the
elimination of Zionism in Palestine." The whole Arab nation
must mobilize to achieve this goal. "The liberation of Palestine,"
states Article 22, "will destroy the Zionist and imperialist presence and will contribute to the establishment of peace in the
Middle East." Israel is defined as "the instrument of the Zionist
movement, and [the] geographical base for world imperialism
placed strategically in the midst of the Arab homeland to combat
the hopes of the Arab nation for liberation, unity and progress.
Israel is a constant source of threat vis-à-vis peace in the Middle
East and the whole world."

Article 6—modified and "improved"—now stated: "The Jews
who had normally resided in Palestine until the beginning of the
Zionist invasion will be considered Palestinians." The PLO nor-

mally dated the "beginning" of the Zionist invasion to the Balfour Declaration of November 1917 (though a more rigorous definition, also in common Palestinian use, located the start of Zionism in 1882). Hence, only Jews who had lived in the country permanently before 1917 (or 1882) would be considered citizens of post-Zionist Palestine. Of course, by 1968 few of Israel's 2.5 million Jews had been permanent residents of Palestine before 1917 (or 1882). What was to be done with those still living from among the millions of post-1882 or post-1917 immigrants and their descendants was not explained.

It is worth noting that the charter, in both its original 1964 and its amended 1968 versions, failed to define the nature of the state the PLO intended to establish, beyond the provision for freedom of worship. Only during the 1970s did some Palestinians hesitantly begin to refer, especially when talking to Westerners, to a "democratic Palestine" or a "secular, democratic Palestine" as their objective (of this, more later)—but this goal was never introduced at any time into the charter, perhaps to avoid alienating Muslim believers, to whom both democracy and secularism were anathema.

In recent years, Palestinian advocates in the West began to belittle the charter, because its insistence on destroying Israel and supplanting it with a Palestine Arab state was impolitic and did their cause little good in Western public opinion. Hence, Palestinian-American historian and activist Rashid Khalidi, in *The Iron Cage*, wrote: "The fact is that it [that is, the charter] was amended at different times [Khalidi's mendacious implication here being that it was amended in a positive, two-state direction], that as time went on most Palestinians paid it less and less heed, and that the political programs adopted by successive PNCs progressively contradicted it, was rarely considered by those who had an interest in showing that there had never been any evolution in the Palestinian position."[149] But the fact is that the PNC was and remains the Palestinian national movement's supreme, sovereign body and its resolutions, including the charter, with its various emendations, were, during the subsequent decades, certainly down to the end of the twentieth century, representative of the Palestinian people's sovereign will.

The main constituent party of the PNC, from 1969 onward, was Fatah (and this remains true today). Fatah, a reverse acronym for the Arabic *harakat al-tahrir al-watani-al-filastini* (meaning the Palestinian National Liberation Movement), is also an Arabic word meaning "opening" or "conquest," a term that, for Arabs, connotes the sweeping Muslim Arab conquests ("openings") of the seventh century.

Fatah was founded, according to its leaders, by a group of Palestinian professionals, mostly working in the Gulf States and hailing from refugee camps in the Gaza Strip, in 1958 or 1959. Among the founders were Yasser Arafat, Salah Khalaf, Mahmoud Abbas, and Khalid al-Hassan. In January 1965 it launched its first cross-border raids, from Lebanon and Syria, into Israel, and by 1967–1968, it had emerged as the largest and strongest of the Palestinian resistance (or, in Israeli parlance, terrorist) movements. From 1969 it dominated the PLO. Under Arafat, Fatah and the PLO were to lead the Palestinian struggle against Israel down to the middle of the first decade of the third millennium when, in 2006, Hamas—the acronym in Arabic of *harakat al-muqawama al-islamiyya*, the Islamic Resistance Movement— defeated Fatah in the Palestinian general elections and supplanted it as the Palestinian majority party or movement.

Fatah's ideology was always straightforward and clear. As Anglo-Palestinian historian Yezid Sayigh has put it, Fatah's "ultimate goal," from inception, "was . . . to destroy . . . Israel as an economic, political, and military entity and restore Palestine as it still existed in the minds of most Palestinians, the [Arab] homeland that was before 1948 . . . There was little difference between Fatah and any other Palestinian group in this respect (with the solitary exception of the communists [who, directed from Moscow, supported a two-state solution]). There was little room for the Jews in this outlook."[150] A Fatah tract from 1967 that Sayigh quotes stated: "[The] military defeat [of Israel] is not the only aim of the Palestinian liberation war, but also elimination of the Zionist character of the occupied homeland, both human and social."[151]

Fatah's ideology is embodied in "The Fatah Constitution," drawn up by the movement in 1964. It has never been revoked or amended. Article 1 states that "Palestine is part of the Arab world"; Article 4 that "the Palestinian struggle is part . . . of the world-wide struggle against Zionism, colonialism and international imperialism"; Article 6 that "UN projects, accords and resolutions . . . which undermine the Palestinian people's right in their homeland are illegal and rejected"; Article 7 that "the Zionist movement is racial, colonial and aggressive"; and Article 9 that "liberating Palestine and protecting its holy places is an Arab, religious and human obligation." The constitution defines Fatah's goals (Article 12) as the "complete liberation of Palestine, and [the] eradication of Zionist economic, political, military and cultural existence" and (Article 13) "establishing an independent democratic state with complete sovereignty on all Palestinian lands, and Jerusalem is its capital city, and protecting the citizens' legal and equal rights without any racial or religious discrimination." Armed struggle is posited as the means for "liberating Palestine . . . [and] uprooting the Zionist existence . . . [and] demolishing the Zionist occupation." ("Occupation" here refers to those areas that became the State of Israel in 1948–1949, not to the territories conquered by the IDF in 1967.) This struggle "will not cease," states Article 19, "unless the Zionist state is demolished and Palestine is completely liberated." (The constitution, of course, also posits the establishment of a "progressive" society, the necessity of "self-criticism" and a "collective leadership," the desire to achieve "international peace," the need for "[non-]discrimination against women," and so on.)[152]

What should happen to the Jews living in "Palestine" (Israel) was nowhere explained. But clearly Fatah's leaders had some level of expulsionist intent. As Salah Khalaf ("Abu Iyad") put it (in *A Dialogue about the Principal Issues*), hinting, or more than hinting, at the goal, the movement had asked the Arab states "to allow former Jewish nationals to reclaim their citizenship and property, with the aim of opening a floodgate for 'reverse emigration' from Israel."[153] Kamal 'Udwan, another Fatah leader, also spoke of pushing the Jews "into reverse emigration," though he added, somewhat contradictorily, that the "option of comprehensive cleansing [is] unacceptable in historic, human and civilizational terms."[154]

In 1970 Yasser Arafat said that the movement's aim was to liberate Palestine "from [the Mediterranean] sea to [the Jordan] river, and from Rafah to Naqura [on the Lebanese border]."[155] But the years wore on, and no liberation was in sight. Following the October 1973 War, the PLO began to moderate its position tactically, if not strategically. The Palestinians were under pressure from the moderate Arab states, led by Anwar Sadat's Egypt, who was headed for peace with Israel, and the West. At issue was whether the PLO should agree to establish a ministate in the West Bank and Gaza Strip should Israel agree to withdraw from these territories as a result of Israeli-Egyptian negotiations or an international peace conference. The Palestinian hard-liners feared that some might interpret Palestinian agreement to establish such a ministate as a statement of inability or unwillingness to continue the struggle to liberate the rest of Palestine; in effect, that the Palestinians were at last making do with, or accepting the principle of, partition and a two-state solution.

Not so, said Arafat, the PLO's chairman and Haj Amin al-Husseini's heir as the leader of the Palestinian national movement. The Palestinians should accept and establish their state on any part of Palestine relinquished by Israel; but this would be only the first stage in what was, and should be regarded as, a phased struggle. "The fourth Arab-Israeli war [the October 1973 War] will give us parts of Palestine, and the fifth war will give us Tel Aviv . . . What is called the West Bank and Gaza Strip . . . now face two possibilities: one, to go to King Hussein [that is, Jordan] . . . as to the second possibility, it is to set up a Palestinian authority on it . . . [If we do this] we will lose some present positions [in Arab countries], but *we will head for our motherland* [in other words, it will bring us closer to our goal, the liberation of the whole motherland]"—through a "policy of phases," as Fatah's Khalid al-Hassan put it.[156]

The idea of a phased struggle to achieve the gradual elimination of Israel and a one (Arab)-state solution was enshrined in the Palestine National Council resolutions of 8 June 1974. These asserted the Palestinians' "national rights" as "rights to [a refugee] return and to self-determination on the whole of the soil of their homeland." The document posited the establishment of a Palestinian polity—or "combatant national authority"—in any territory "liberated" from or vacated by Israel and committed the PLO to oppose any "Palestinian entity the price of which is recognition, peace, secure frontiers [for Israel], [or] renunciation of national rights." The document clarified the "phased" approach to achieving the national goals: "Any step taken towards liberation is a step towards the realization of the Liberation Organization's strategy of establishing the democratic Palestinian State specified in the resolutions of the previous Palestinian National Councils [that is, the PNC resolutions of 1964 and 1968] . . . Once it is established, the Palestinian national authority will strive to achieve a union of the confrontation countries, with the aim of completing the liberation of all Palestinian territory."[157] Or as Salah Khalaf, Arafat's deputy, put it: "What were the mistakes of our previous leaders? Their mistake was adhering to our people's historical rights without adopting stage-by-stage programs of struggle."[158] And in interviews, Arafat continued to enunciate the traditional policy of "no concession of our historic rights," "no reconciliation," "no negotiations," no recognition of Israel, and no peace.[159]

Fatah-linked Palestinian historians and spokesmen in the West have generally described the 1974 resolutions as a "shift in objectives"—from one-statism to two-statism—"[that] was entirely genuine for most Palestinians . . . [or such as] appeared to satisfy most Palestinians."[160] And Western commentators sympathetic to the Palestinians have over the years latched onto the resolutions as signaling the beginning of—or even the complete

and final—acceptance by the PLO of a two-state solution, leading to the establishment of a small Palestinian Arab state alongside, and coexisting peacefully with, Israel.[161]

But historians familiar with the internal PLO material have
been less upbeat (in terms of two-statism). Yezid Sayigh, the
leading historian of the PLO, wrote: "[The] total liberation of
Palestine presumably remained the genuine desire of most, if not
all its [that is, the PLO's] members, but they were keenly aware
of the regional and international impediments to the destruction
of Israel." In other words, they adopted a conciliatory face to appease the West, but in effect, Arafat and company saw 1974
merely as the acceptance of the need for the elimination of Israel
in stages rather than in one fell swoop, given the diplomatic and
military realities. As Sayigh phrased it, citing the argument put
by Khalid al-Hassan, one of the Fatah and PLO leaders: "The
PLO faced the hypothetical choice between an indirect, 'phased'
strategy that would see the establishment of a state in the occupied territories as a first stage, and a direct strategy of unrelenting military conflict in which Arab resources would have to be
fully mobilized. The latter option was simply unavailable . . .
The indirect strategy still took the establishment of a secular,
democratic state over the whole of Mandate Palestine as its ultimate goal."[162]

Several months later, Arafat was invited to address the United
Nations General Assembly. In his famous "Gun and Olive Branch
Speech" of 13 November 1974 (he stood at the podium with a

holstered gun at his hip), Arafat lambasted Zionism as "the chief form" of racism in the world: "it is united with anti-Semitism in its retrograde tenets." And he laid out his vision: "[I] dream [of] a peaceful future in Palestine's sacred land . . . Let us work together that my dream may be fulfilled, that I may return with my people out of exile . . . there in Palestine to live . . . in one democratic State where Christian, Jew and Muslim live in justice, equality and fraternity. As chairman of the PLO . . . I proclaim . . . that when we speak of our common hopes for the Palestine of tomorrow we include in our perspective all Jews now living in Palestine who choose to live with us there in peace and without discrimination."

Arafat thus appeared to have dropped the National Charter's stipulation about Jews resident in Palestine after 1917. But, while Palestinian propagandists at the time were busy telling the world that the PLO was beginning to accept the notion of a two-state compromise, Arafat was reiterating the PLO's traditional one-state goal, albeit dicing it up as a "democratic" polity.

Arafat concluded his speech with a warning: "I have come bearing an olive branch and a freedom-fighter's gun. Do not let the olive branch fall from my hand."[163]

Three years later, on 22 March 1977, during a lull in the Lebanese civil war, after a bout of PLO-Syrian fighting, the PNC implicitly reendorsed its willingness to establish a ministate in any part of Palestine vacated by Israel—but reaffirmed the Palestinian resolve to liberate "all the occupied Arab land" (meaning all of Palestine) and restore the "permanent national rights of the Palestinian nation, without peace [with Israel] or recognition [of Israel]."[164]

Through the 1970s, the rejectionist Palestinian groups, such as the Popular Front for the Liberation of Palestine and the Islamists, continued to oppose the PNC's enunciated phased approach and the establishment of a temporary Palestinian ministate as the first step toward "liberating the whole of Palestine."[165] And following Sadat's November 1977 visit to Jerusalem, the PLO formally joined, or rejoined, them and returned to the bosom of the "steadfastness and confrontation front," composed of rejectionist Syria, Libya, and other Arab states that officially and openly sought Israel's destruction. The meeting of the rejectionist states (and the PLO) in Tripoli on 2–5 December, in its concluding resolution, denounced Sadat, rejected UN Security Council Resolutions 242 and 338, and reiterated the "no peace, no recognition, and no negotiation" formula adopted by the Arab League at Khartoum in 1967. Salah Khalaf signed the resolution for Fatah, Hamid Abu-Sitta for the PLO; Arafat, always the agile operator, stayed away from the signing ceremony.

But his inclinations and position were clear. In Beirut in December 1980 he told a meeting: "When we speak of the Palestinians' return, we want to say: Acre before Gaza, Beersheba before Hebron. We recognize one thing, namely that the Palestinian flag will fly over Jaffa."[166] Acre, Beersheba, and Jaffa—unlike

Gaza and Hebron—are parts of Israel proper, indeed deep in Israel, in its pre-1967 configuration.

During the 1970s and early 1980s, a number of PLO dissidents—and here we appear to be talking about real as opposed to make-believe PLO "moderates"—struck out on their own, secretly "negotiating" or, rather, debating with left-wing Israelis, and hesitantly raising the idea of a two-state solution (usually based on the UN General Assembly Resolution 181 borders, that is, the partition resolution of November 1947). But all were gunned down, ad seriatim, by their less moderate Palestinian colleagues. The best known were Said Hamami, the PLO representative in London, murdered on 4 January 1978, 'Izz al-Din Kalak, murdered on 3 August 1978, and Issam Sartawi, murdered on 10 April 1983.

DID THE PLO SUBSEQUENTLY ACCEPT A TWO-STATE SOLUTION?
In 1982 Israeli troops invaded Southern Lebanon and besieged West Beirut, shattering the PLO as a military force. Arafat and his remaining cadres and troops were forced to leave Beirut and reestablish themselves far from Palestine, in Tunis, Yemen, and other sites in the Arab world. Five years later, the inhabitants of the occupied West Bank and Gaza Strip rose in semiarmed revolt against Israel, a revolt or intifada (in Arabic, a shaking-off, as a dog shakes off a flea) that ended only four to five years later. The two events, the first by weakening the PLO and weakening in-

ternational support for it, and the second by unleashing popular Palestinian pressure from the West Bank and Gaza Strip on the exiled PLO leadership to moderate its positions, resulted in the 15 November 1988 "Palestinian Declaration of Independence," formulated by the PNC. It was preceded by a "trial balloon," launched by Arafat's aide Bassam Abu Sharif, who in June that year publicly called for a "two-state" solution and "lasting peace" based on mutual recognition.[167]

The text of the Declaration of Independence was apparently written largely by the leading Palestinian poet, Mahmoud Darwish, normally resident in Paris. The English-language translation was drafted by Edward Said, the leading Palestinian American academic.

During the PNC deliberations in Algiers before the publication of the declaration, in the keynote address on 14 November, Arafat's deputy, Salah Khalaf, reiterated the PLO's policy of a phased takeover of all of Palestine: "This is a state for the coming generations. At first, [the Palestinian state] would be small . . . [But] God willing, it would expand eastward, westward, northward, and southward . . . [True,] I [once] wanted all of Palestine all at once. But I was a fool. Yes, I am interested in the liberation of Palestine, but the question is how. And the answer is: Step by step."[168]

To the West, the PLO presented the Declaration of Independence as a radical moderation of its positions. The declaration referred to UN General Assembly Resolution 181, "which partitioned Palestine into two states, one Arab, one Jewish," viewing the resolution as the international warrant and grant of legitimacy for "the right of the Palestinian Arab people to sovereignty" (whereas previous PNC and PLO statements had always dismissed the resolution as "null and void," because it also underpinned Israel's right to exist). The declaration referred to the Palestinian "patrimony," "rights," including to self-determination, and "territory." It nowhere asserted the Palestinian claim to all of Palestine. But at the same time, the declaration refrained from defining geographically "The State of Palestine," whose independence was now being proclaimed; even more tellingly, nowhere was the State of Israel mentioned or described. The document rejected the use of violence against Palestinian "territorial integrity and independence" much as it rejected the use of violence "against [the] territorial integrity of other states" (Israel was not specified). The declaration rededicated the Palestinian people to the struggle that "shall continue until the occupation ends"—but whether the reference was to the West Bank and Gaza Strip (occupied since 1967) alone or to all of Jewish-occupied Palestine, the normal usage of the word "occupation" in Palestinian discourse since 1949, was left unclear. The declaration ended with an invocation of Allah, "the Compassionate, the Merciful":

> Say: O God, Master of the Kingdom,
> Thou givest the Kingdom to whom Thou wilt,

And seizes the Kingdom from whom Thou wilt,
Thou exalted whom Thou wilt, and Thou
Abasest whom Thou wilt; in Thy hand
Is the good; Thou art powerful over everything.[169]

Many Westerners and some Israelis saw the document as implying acceptance of Israel's existence—and Palestinian spokesmen in the West, bent on winning over hearts and minds, described it thus: "This was the first official Palestinian recognition of the legitimacy of the existence of a Jewish state, and the first unequivocal, explicit PLO endorsement of a two-state solution to the conflict."[170] But of course, it was no such thing.

Nevertheless, during the following decade, the PLO appeared to inch significantly toward a two-state solution and acceptance of Israel's legitimacy. On 13 December 1988, speaking before the UN General Assembly convened in Geneva, Arafat spoke of making "peace based on justice." But he failed to address Israel's right to exist or to dispel the ambiguities relating to UN Security Council Resolutions 242 and 338, which provided the accepted international basis for a negotiated peace. Two days later, at a press conference, Arafat declared that the PNC had accepted Resolutions 242 and 338 as a basis for negotiations—in truth, it had not—and he renounced "all types of terrorism." During the following months, Arafat—located between a rock (PLO rejectionist-eliminationist ideology vis-à-vis Israel) and a hard place (American and West Bank–Gaza Palestinian demands for a moderation of the PLO's position)—continued to play duplici-tous word games. For example, in May 1989 Arafat told a French interviewer, "C'est caduc" (It is null and void), speaking of the Palestinian National Charter, which called for Israel's destruc-tion. The Israelis and the Americans were unpersuaded, if only because the PNC alone had the authority to change or revoke the charter, and it had not done so.

But then things began, or seemingly began, to change. In Oc-tober 1991, under American pressure, representatives of Israel and the Arab states convoked in a peace conference in Madrid. For the first time, PLO delegates, albeit "soft" ones, without military or terroristic résumés and lightly camouflaged as part of a joint Jordanian-Palestinian delegation, took part in talks with Israel. The conference came to naught, but in June 1992 Israel's Labor Party, with Yitzhak Rabin at the helm, won power—it was a resounding expression, after years of Likud governance, of the will of the Israeli electorate for a peace based on territorial com-promise—and a few months later, Israeli and PLO represen-tatives launched secret peace talks, without American involve-ment, in Norway. By May 1993 the main lines of an agreement had gelled, and in September, Israel and the PLO exchanged let-ters of mutual recognition. Arafat wrote Rabin on 9 September that the PLO "recognize[s] the right of the State of Israel to exist in peace and security," "accepts UN Security Council resolu-tions 242 and 338," commits itself "to a peaceful resolution of the conflict," "renounces the use of terrorism" and affirms that the articles in the charter that denied Israel's right to exist "are now inoperative and no longer valid." Arafat undertook "to submit to the Palestinian National Council . . . the necessary changes in regard to the Palestinian Charter." In response, Rabin sent a brief letter stating that "the Government of Israel has decided to recognize the PLO as the representative of the Palestinian people" and to negotiate peace with it.[171]

The secret negotiations and the exchange of letters in which they culminated marked the start of the Israeli-Palestinian Oslo peace process, which was to dominate Middle Eastern politics until 2000. On 13 September 1993 Rabin and Arafat, on the White House lawn, with US president Bill Clinton as witness, signed the Declaration of Principles. The two sides agreed to put an end to the conflict, "recognize their mutual legitimate and political rights . . . and achieve a just, lasting and comprehensive peace." Israel agreed to a gradual devolution of power in the territories and an initial withdrawal from much of the Gaza Strip and the Jericho area in the West Bank, and, within three years of this devolution of power, to enter into negotiations for a final status agreement, covering refugees, borders, Jerusalem, settlements, security, and Palestinian statehood.

During the following months—which were dotted by fundamentalist Islamic terrorist attacks inside Israel and a major attack by a fundamentalist Jew, the slaughter by Baruch Goldstein, at the Tomb of the Patriarchs in Hebron (the Ibrahimiyya Mosque) on 25 February 1994, of twenty-nine Muslim worshippers, all aimed at torpedoing the peace process—the Israelis and the PLO signed a series of interim agreements. More powers were awarded the newly created Palestine National Authority, and the traditional old guard leadership of the PLO was allowed to return from exile in Tunis to the territories. Most major West Bank towns (Ramallah, Tulkarm, Nablus, Jenin, Bethlehem) were transferred to the control of the newly established PNA security forces.

But Arafat kept dropping hints, in speeches in Arabic to Muslim audiences, that he was still wedded to the phased policy of liberating all of Palestine and had no intention of honoring a two-state settlement. He turned a blind eye to continued Palestinian terrorism and occasionally encouraged it. On 10 May 1994 he delivered a sermon (in broken English) in a mosque in Johannesburg, South Africa, in which he promised that "the *jihad* will continue." Not "the permanent State of Israel" but "the permanent State of Palestine" is what is under discussion with the Israelis, he assured his listeners. In any event, he added, for him the Oslo Accord was no more binding than the accord signed by Muhammad with the Quraish tribe in 628 in Hijaz, "Hudnat Hudeibiya (the Hudeibiya truce)," which provided for a ten-year ceasefire between the faithful and the infidel tribe, which Muhammad proceeded to violate less than two years later, once his forces were ready.[172]

After 1993, once the PLO was firmly ensconced in the territories, Israel was subjected to continuous terrorist attack by Islamic fundamentalists and PLO-linked forces—in violation of the agreements signed by Arafat and his aides. These resulted in Israeli foot-dragging in implementing its side of the Oslo commitments. Ultimately, Palestinian terrorism strengthened Israel's right and assured the election of Benjamin Netanyahu, the Likud leader, rather than Labor's Shimon Peres, as prime minister in the 1996 general elections, which followed the November 1995 assassination of Yitzhak Rabin by a right-wing Israeli law student.

The Netanyahu years, 1996–1999, were a period of paralysis in the peace process—curiously marred by far fewer Arab terrorist attacks than the previous years of peace-minded Labor administration (probably due to the close and effective anti-Hamas cooperation between Israel's and the PNA's security forces)—though Israel grudgingly added most of the city of Hebron to the territory controlled by the PNA. The PNA, for its part, after protracted foot-dragging and American and Israeli pressures, made good, or appeared to make good, on its commitment of 1993 regarding the charter. On 24 April 1996 the PNC met in Gaza and, by a vote of 504 to 54, with 14 abstentions, decided to amend the charter in line with Arafat's commitments to excise the articles calling for Israel's destruction. The resolution also authorized the PLO's legal committee to redraft the charter and present the new version to the PLO Central Committee.

But two problems have obtruded. The first is simple: the PNA/PLO failed during the following thirteen years to "redraft"

and ratify an amended charter or adopt a new, alternative charter, which omits the articles endorsing Israel's destruction. The
second is more complicated and bears directly on Palestinian
mendacity, which has accompanied the shifts and turns in Palestinian politics and diplomacy vis-à-vis Israel since the 1970s.
The official Palestinian translation into English of the first part
of the 24 April resolution read: "The Palestinian National Charter is hereby amended by canceling the articles that are contrary
to the letters exchanged between the PLO and the Government
of Israel 9–10 September 1993." But the earlier Palestinian version of the translation, posted on the official PNA web site,
stated that the PNC had "decided to change/amend" the charter,
meaning that the PNC intended at some point in the future to
amend the charter, not that it had "hereby amended" the charter.
And neither version specified what exactly was to be amended or
had been amended.

So, quite naturally, many PLO stalwarts insisted that the charter had not, in fact, been changed. Farouk Kaddoumi, the PLO's
long-time rejectionist "foreign minister" who lives in Tunis, in
an interview with a Jordanian newspaper in 2004 put it this way:
"The Palestinian National Charter has not been amended . . . It
was said that some articles are no longer effective, but they were
not changed."[173]

So, quite naturally, the Netanyahu government continued to
complain and press Arafat, directly and via Washington, regarding the necessary emendation of the charter. The upshot was

Arafat's letters of January 1998 to President Clinton and British prime minister Tony Blair. Arafat wrote Clinton that the PNC in April 1996 had decided that the charter "is hereby amended by canceling the articles that are contrary" to the Rabin-Arafat letters of September 1993 and went on to list the articles that had been nullified or partly nullified, which were "inconsistent with the PLO commitment to recognize and live in peace side by side with Israel."[174] But neither Netanyahu nor the Americans were mollified. Arafat needed to take one further step.

The matter was (apparently) resolved during Clinton's brief visit to Gaza on 14 December 1998, when by a show of hands the gathered members of the PNC, the PLO Central Council, PNA ministers, and Arafat voted overwhelmingly to endorse the PNC resolution of 1996, after which Clinton declared: "I thank you for your rejection—fully, finally and forever—of the passages in the Palestinian Charter calling for the destruction of Israel. For they were the ideological underpinning of a struggle renounced at Oslo."[175]

Still, the six years of Palestinian foot-dragging and squiggling over the charter—important both as symbol and as substance—had left many Israelis skeptical. After all, the PNA and PLO, under Arafat (and then under his successor as Palestinian president, Mahmoud Abbas) had failed to produce a new, appropriately modified charter, as they originally had promised. Did their obvious reluctance to carry out these commitments not hint at the basic untrustworthiness of Israel's "partners" in peace? Did

Arafat and the PNC really accept a two-state solution, and even if so, did they really represent the will of the Palestinian national movement? What were the Palestinians really after?

2000 AND AFTER

To a degree, all these questions arose with reinvigorated anguish two years later, in 2000, with the failure of the Camp David summit in July, the Clinton peace proposals of 23 December and their reception, and the outbreak of the Second Intifada in between, in late September. Had the Palestinian national movement really abandoned its one-state goal?

As with 1937 and 1947, the year 2000 represented a milestone in the Palestinian approach to a solution to the conflict. But, in a sense, it was a more defining milestone than its predecessors. For in 1937 and 1947, in rejecting the two-state solutions proposed, respectively, by the Peel Commission and the UN General Assembly, the Palestinian Arabs had merely been expressing their consistently held and publicized attitude toward a resolution of the conflict; only a one-state solution, a Palestinian Arab state with a minuscule, disempowered Jewish minority, was acceptable. In rejecting the two-state solution offered, in two versions, in 2000, they were also—so it seemed—reneging on a process and on a commitment they had made, and repeated, in the course of the 1990s. And whereas in 1937 and 1947 they had rejected merely a two-state vision, a possibility, as it were, in 2000 they were also rejecting a reality, denying the legitimacy and right to life of an existing state, subverting a principle on which the international order rests. Hence the surprise and shock of peace-mongering Israelis and well-meaning Westerners—a surprise and shock that had been completely absent in 1937 and 1947 among Arab, Zionist, and British observers.

Some of the details about the negotiations of 2000, and the interpretation of their meaning, are in heated dispute. But the factual bare bones of what happened in July, September–October, and December 2000 are simple.

In early summer 2000, after the replacement in general elections the year before of the recalcitrant Netanyahu by Labor's Ehud Barak, and after years of salami-style Israeli-Palestinian negotiation on the margins of the core issues, Clinton, prodded by Barak, decided to take the bull by the horns. Clinton invited the Israeli and Palestinian leaderships to the closed-off venue of Camp David to hammer out a final, comprehensive deal.

The Palestinians were somewhat wary, saying that they were "unprepared"; and they feared that the Israelis and Americans, who were allies, would "gang up" on them. And Barak was hobbled by a disintegrating government: three of his right-wing and religious coalition partners (Shas, the National Religious Party, and Yisrael Ba'aliya), opposed to his expected concessions on territory and Jerusalem, bolted the government in the days before he departed for the United States. (This fact would later enable Palestinians and their supporters to argue that whatever Barak had offered had been meaningless because he would never have been able to deliver on it. But the Israelis countered with a precedent: had Barak and Arafat reached a deal, the Israeli public would have given Barak a wholesome mandate, overruling the recalcitrant political party leaderships—much as had occurred in 1978–1979, when the public, and in its wake, the great majority of its parliamentary representatives, had supported Begin after he had concluded the deal with Sadat, in which Israel gave up the Sinai Peninsula in exchange for peace with Egypt.)

But who can refuse an American presidential invitation or appear to turn down what is promoted as a last, "make or break," chance for peace? The parties convened in Camp David on 11 July. Clinton, in advance, assured Arafat—as the Palestinians demanded—that he would not publicly blame anyone if the summit collapsed. In the nonstop cycle of bilateral one-on-one and trilateral discussions that followed, between Arafat and Barak, with Clinton mediating and bridging gaps, and between teams of aides, the major issues were tackled and some gaps were narrowed. At base, Barak put on the table an offer of a Palestinian state in exchange for peace. Israel made a series of proposals, each better than the last, on territory, Jerusalem, the nature of the Palestinian state. Arafat consistently said "no" and demanded more. He made no proposals or offers of his own and, after occasionally hinting (through aides) at a willingness to concede a point on this or that issue, quickly withdrew the concession, saying he had been misunderstood. (Arafat's English was poor—and he exploited this to parry, obfuscate, and bamboozle.) Barak, for his part, offered nothing in writing and presented no maps, later arguing that he had not wanted to leave the Palestinians with a series of concrete Israeli concessions in hand—which would then have served as the starting point in a future round of negotiations—if the Palestinians offered no concessions of their own and Camp David collapsed. But, as a result, the Palestinians could—and would—later argue that Barak had not really offered them anything, or anything concrete.

The contemporary official American, Israeli, and Arab documentation is of course still classified. But recollections of the discussions, based on real-time notes and diary entries, by Clinton and Dennis Ross, the chief American Middle East negotiator, and by Gilead Sher and Shlomo Ben-'Ami, Barak's aides, were published in short order, as were a variety of interviews and articles. Hence, a reasonably accurate idea of what was discussed and what was offered by Israel, under constant American prodding, and what was rejected or what was not offered by Arafat, despite American prodding, has emerged.[176]

Barak offered Arafat the establishment of an independent, but essentially demilitarized, Palestinian Arab state in the Gaza Strip and the bulk of the West Bank, with its capital in East Jerusalem. Barak said that Israel would withdraw its troops and settlers from the whole of the Gaza Strip. At the start of the summit, he said that about 80 percent of the West Bank would revert to Palestinian sovereignty; by its end, 90–91 percent was offered (and the equivalent of 1 percent compensation to the Palestinians from Israeli territory proper). Barak said that Israel would retain the remaining 9–10 percent of the territory along the Green Line, with the thick clusters of Jewish settlements (the 'Etzion Bloc, Ariel, and so on), and the settlers inhabiting the core areas of the West Bank and the Gaza Strip would be pulled back and resettled in these blocs. Israel would retain, at least temporarily, a thin strip of the southern Jordan Valley along the river as a security zone. It is not clear whether, at the end of the summit, Israel still insisted on retaining another thin strip of territory running from Jerusalem through Ma'ale Adumim to the Jordan River, which, Barak at one point explained, the Palestinians could traverse with tunnels or bridges to maintain contiguity between the northern (Ramallah-Nablus-Jenin) and southern (Bethlehem-Hebron-Dhahiriya) sections of the West Bank.[177]

As to Jerusalem, Barak—breaking a long-held Israeli taboo regarding the redivision of the ("unified") city—offered the Palestinians sovereignty over the outlying Arab neighborhoods and some form of functional control in the core Arab neighborhoods. The Palestinians were also to get control of part of the Old City, with some characteristics of sovereignty, and control though not sovereignty over the Temple Mount (*al-haram al-sharif*, the noble sanctuary), containing al-Aksa Mosque and the Dome of the Rock. There was to be a Palestinian "right of return" to the territory of the future Palestinian state but not to Israel (though

Barak agreed to full compensation of the refugees for their lost property and hinted at a readiness to absorb in Israel a token number of elderly refugees within a "family reunion" scheme).

Arafat rejected the offered two-state solution. Ross recorded that Clinton blew up and yelled at the PLO leader that he had "been here fourteen days and said no to everything."[178] Or as Clinton put it in his memoirs: on Day 8 of the summit Arafat "turned the offer down"; on Day 9, "I gave Arafat my best shot again" and "again he said no"; on Day 13, "Again Arafat said no. I shut down the talks. It was frustrating and profoundly sad."[179] Arafat had demanded all 100 percent of the Gaza Strip and West Bank (though at one point one of his aides spoke of a readiness to cede 2–3 percent of the West Bank, with equivalent Israeli cession of territory to the Palestinians elsewhere); sovereignty over all of East Jerusalem and its Old City, except the Wailing Wall (or, in a variant, the Wailing Wall and the Jewish Quarter), and full, sole Palestinian Arab sovereignty over the Temple Mount. Indeed, at one point Arafat denied that there had ever been a Temple Mount in Jerusalem. He rejected Clinton's last-minute proposal that sovereignty in the Old City be divided, with the Arabs sovereign over the Muslim and Christian quarters and the Jews sovereign in the rest (the Jewish and Armenian quarters), and that the Palestinians receive "custodianship" over the Temple Mount, but without full, formal sovereignty.[180] Arafat also demanded Israeli acceptance of the principle of the "right of return" and agreement to the return of the refugees to their pre-1948 homes and lands in Israel proper.

The summit broke up in failure on 26 July. Recriminations followed. Clinton, contrary to his presummit assurances, and Barak both blamed Arafat and his inflexibility for the failure and expressed astonishment that the Arabs had rejected the most far-reaching Israeli concessions ever made. For years, the Palestinians had been demanding a two-state solution; for years, Israel had stalled—even Rabin had not formally endorsed two "states." Now, at last, when Israel (and the United States) offered it, the Palestinians turned it down. Arafat and his aides lambasted Israel for making inadequate proposals, which amounted to giving the Palestinians a cluster of "bantustans" rather than a full-fledged independent state—and this on less than 20 percent of the territory of Mandate Palestine (the Palestinians argued that, in effect, they had already made a major "concession" in accepting the loss of the 78–79 percent of Palestine on which Israel was established in 1948–1949). There were frustration and disappointment in the Palestinian public—which was misinformed by its leaders and media about what exactly the Israelis had offered—and among left-wing Israelis, most of whom felt that they had reached the limit of concession and had been rebuffed.

Further Israeli-Palestinian talks followed. But no breakthrough was achieved, and on 28 September the Likud's new leader, Ariel Sharon, guarded by dozens of policemen, visited the Temple Mount for twenty-four minutes in what many Arabs regarded as a provocation (though he made no statement and did not enter the mosques). Muslim crowds gathered in Jerusalem and began pelting the police with stones. The following day, a Friday, tens of thousands gathered on the Temple Mount for prayers, and large-scale riots erupted. The rioting quickly spread to the West Bank and Gaza, and Israeli and Palestinian security men exchanged fire. Palestinian broadcasters and leaders invoked jihad. The Second Intifada had begun.

It is unclear whether the PNA and Arafat had deliberately ignited the violence or had, in a more general way, prepared the hearts and minds of the inhabitants of the West Bank and Gaza Strip for its commencement (without actually ordering its start on the day and hour it began), or whether it had broken out completely spontaneously but had then been inflamed by specific, local Israeli overreactions (or underreactions) to the violence and by deliberate PNA incitement, with Arafat, as it were, riding and, in various ways, guiding the tiger. What is clear is that Arafat and his aides did nothing to douse the flames while occasionally pretending, vis-à-vis Washington, that they were trying to.

The Americans moved to curb the eruption. By mid-December they had readied a comprehensive bridging proposal of their own (after first receiving a degree of assent to its terms from Barak). Some critics then and later were to argue that Clinton should have formulated and presented his proposals at the start or in the course of Camp David, and not waited until December.

Be that as it may, on 23 December Clinton met Palestinian

and Israeli representatives and handed them and published his "Parameters" or proposals for an Israeli-Palestinian peace. He stipulated that the parameters must be accepted or rejected as a package—they included trade-offs in concessions by both sides— and in principle within four days. Each side could then negotiate details "within" the bounds of the parameters; but regarding the principles, it was a take it or leave it offer. The parameters were nonnegotiable.

The Clinton proposals, offering a two-state settlement, stipulated that Israel must withdraw from between 94 and 96 percent of the West Bank and, implicitly, 100 percent of the Gaza Strip, in which the Palestinian Arab state would then be established. Israel would compensate the Palestinians for the loss of the 4–6 percent of the West Bank that they would be "ceding" with a patch of Israeli territory amounting to "1 to 3 percent" of the West Bank as well as allowing the Palestinians a "safe passage" corridor between Gaza and the West Bank through Israeli territory. The 4–6 percent of the West Bank retained by Israel would include the large settlement concentrations, such as the 'Etzion Bloc, which held some 80 percent of the territory's settlers.

The Israeli withdrawal from the Palestinian territories should be phased over thirty-six months, with an "international presence" overseeing the process. Israel would retain a "small military presence" in the Jordan Valley for "another 36 months." Israel would also retain three early warning facilities in the West Bank, subject to review after ten years. A possible "emergency deployment" of Israeli forces in the Jordan Valley (in case of a threat developing from the east) and their routes of passage through the West Bank would need to be negotiated, as would the Israelis' use of Palestinian air space for training and operations.

The Palestinian state that would be established should be "non-militarised," but with a "strong Palestinian security force." An international force would secure the future Palestine-Israel border.

Jerusalem should be divided along ethnic lines. Arab-populated districts should be under Arab sovereignty and Jewish districts under Israeli sovereignty: "This would apply to the Old City as well."

As to the Temple Mount, Clinton proposed "to formalise the Palestinian *de facto* control over the Haram, while respecting the convictions of the Jewish people." This could be done by giving the Palestinians "sovereignty over the Haram and . . . [Israel] sovereignty over the Western Wall and the space sacred to Judaism of which it is a part" or over "the Western Wall and the holy of holies of which it is a part." Alternatively, there could be "Palestinian sovereignty over the Haram and Israeli sovereignty over the Western Wall and 'shared functional sovereignty over the issue of excavation under the Haram or behind the Wall.'" Any excavation "beneath the Haram or behind the Western Wall" would require "mutual consent."

What this oblique language meant was that the Jews would

have sovereignty over the Western Wall and some manner of control or sovereignty over the interior of the Temple Mount that presumably contains the remains of the Jewish First and Second temples while the Arabs would have sovereignty over the mount's surface area, on which sit the two sacred mosques. Such a formulation met the Palestinian demand for sovereignty over the Haram and the Jewish demand that irresponsible excavation below the surface by the Muslims controlling the Mount be prevented. In effect, Clinton was saying that Islam (the PNA) and Judaism (Israel) would have to compromise and somehow share sovereignty over that holiest of sites.

As to the refugees, Clinton proposed that Israel "acknowledge the moral and material suffering caused to the Palestinian people as a result of the 1948 war" and that "compensation, resettlement [and] rehabilitation" of the refugees enjoy massive international assistance. Regarding the question of the "Right of Return," Clinton said he understood both "how hard it is for the Palestinian leadership to appear to be abandoning this principle" and, for the Israelis, the impossibility of accepting the "right [of Arabs] to immigrate to Israel . . . that would [demographically] threaten the Jewish character of the state." Hence, the solution lay in "the two-state approach" of having a "State of Palestine as the homeland for the Palestinian [Arab] people and the State of Israel as the homeland for the Jewish people." What this meant, in practice, was that the Palestinian refugees would have the right of return to the Palestinian state "without ruling out that Israel would accept some of these refugees"—though not a sizable number such as would threaten the Jewish character of Israel. Clinton suggested that the two sides "recognize the right of the Palestinian refugees to return" either to "their historic homeland" or "to their homeland" and that the refugees either resettle in their host countries, resettle in the Palestinian state or in third countries, or move to Israel but that any return to Israel "would depend upon" Israeli agreement. The two parties would have to agree that this formula represented implementation of UN General Assembly Resolution 194, of December 1948, the resolution to which the Palestinians anchored their insistence on "the right of return."

Clinton said that an agreement based on these parameters would mark "the end of the conflict and its implementation [would] put an end to all claims." He expressed readiness to continue negotiations with the leaders "based on these ideas" and stated that if they were not accepted, they would be "not just off the table" when his presidency ended the following month (January 2001) but gone completely.[181]

On the night of 27–28 December 2000 the Israeli cabinet voted to accept the Clinton parameters. The statement issued after the meeting and transmitted to Washington on 28 December said: "Israel sees these ideas as a basis for discussion provided that they remain unchanged as a basis for discussion also by the Palestinian side."[182]

On 5 January the Israelis transmitted to Washington a more

formal acceptance of the parameters, which included reservations and clarifications. The Israelis praised "the President's ideas as a courageous attempt to offer the Parties principles and guidelines for a Framework Agreement on Permanent Status." Concluding an agreement on this basis would entail historic concessions on the part of both the Israelis and the Palestinians and "Israel would be forced to confront a tremendously difficult rupture, or ruptures, among its citizens."

The Israeli response was embodied in a three-page letter from Gilead Sher, Barak's chef de bureau, to Samuel Berger, the American national security adviser, with an appended three-page note entitled "Points of Clarification." The letter and note (unlike the Arab response to the parameters) were never published.

In the letter, Israel expressed unhappiness with the "numerical territorial values"—that is, the 4–6 percent to be ceded to Israel from the West Bank—and deemed them "insufficient"; but it did not explicitly demand more or suggest an alternative figure. The Israelis also requested "further elaboration" regarding the "sovereign and functional arrangements in and around Har Habayit" (that is, the Temple Mount) "to take adequate account of the 3,000-year ties of Judaism to the site." In the "Points of Clarification" they added that as "the fundamental principle underlying the President's ideas" was that "what is holy to Islam shall be under Palestinian sovereignty and what is holy to Judaism shall be under Israeli sovereignty," the Western Wall and "the space sacred to the Jews . . . should be understood to incorporate the

Kotel [that is, Western Wall] Tunnel, the Mahkame [a nearby building], the Kotel [that is, the Western Wall] itself and the remaining part of the Wall towards [that is, leading to] the South Wall, as well as the Ofel Garden, the City of David, Mount of Olives, and the Tombs of the Kings and Prophets," all areas adjacent to the Temple Mount walls, west, south and east of the mount itself (together referred to as *ha'agan hakadosh*, the Holy Basin). Lastly, the Israelis complained that Clinton's ideas on the refugee issue "embody [a] certain ambiguity, which Israel wishes to avoid."[183]

In Clinton's (and Ross's) view, the Israelis, whatever their misgivings, had said "yes." In his memoirs, Clinton explicitly defined "all [the Israeli] reservations [as falling] within the parameters."[184]

But the Palestinians again said "no." After delaying their response to the proposals beyond the four days allotted by Clinton, the Palestinians presented a set of reservations that together amounted to a flat rejection of the package. The PNA response, dated 1 January 2001, entitled "Remarks and Questions," was accompanied by a letter by Yasser Abed Rabbo, "head of the Palestinian negotiating team," effectively saying "no" to almost each and every parameter. In some instances, the "no" was explicit; in others, it was framed as a "question" or misgivings. But taken in toto, the Palestinian document amounted to a resounding "no."

After cursory expressions of gratitude to Clinton, the Palestinian note stated: "We wish to explain why the latest United

States proposals, taken together and as presented without clarification, fail to satisfy the conditions required for a permanent peace." The parameters, it stated, "divide a Palestinian state into three separate cantons connected and divided by Jewish only and Arab-only roads . . . [d]ivide Palestinian Jerusalem into a number of unconnected islands . . . [and ask] Palestinians to surrender the right of return of Palestinian refugees. [The proposal] also fails to provide workable security arrangements between Palestine and Israel . . . Recognition of the right of return and the provision of choice to refugees [meaning the choice to return to Israeli territory] is a pre-requisite for the closure of the conflict . . . The United States proposal seems to respond to Israeli demands while neglecting the basic Palestinian need: a viable state."

Moving into specifics, the Palestinians charged that the territory of the West Bank dealt with in the parameters excluded the Dead Sea, "no-man's land," and Jerusalem from "the total area from which the percentages are calculated." Moreover, the implication of the "Parameters" was that the Palestinians would not be given Israeli compensation for the ceded West Bank land in a ratio of one to one, and the area Israel proposed to give the Palestinians was "currently being used by Israel to dump toxic waste," in no way comparable to the quality of the West Bank land Israel was being given.[185]

As to the Temple Mount, the Palestinians said that the "formulations" regarding the Haram were "problematic." The Clinton proposals implied recognition of "Israeli sovereignty under the Haram"—which the Palestinians found unacceptable. The implication was that they insisted on full and sole sovereignty over the mount, above and below ground. On this point, the Palestinians, speaking for Islam, refused all compromise or equity.

The Palestinians also implied nonacceptance of an Israeli military presence along the Jordan, even for a limited time, and of "emergency deployment rights"; for both, stated the Palestinians, the Israelis had not made "a persuasive case." Moreover, Israel needed no more than one early warning station "to satisfy its strategic needs." Nor was the idea of Israel having aerial training and operational rights in Palestinian air space acceptable.

Last, of the points specified by Clinton, the Palestinians objected to the "end-of-conflict" clause. "We believe that this can only be achieved once the issues that have caused and perpetrated [sic] the conflict are resolved in full." This seemed to mean, for example, that so long as there were refugees who remained dissatisfied with their lot, or, perhaps, so long as Israel existed, the PNA would not agree to the "end of conflict."

For good measure, the Palestinians added that the parameters failed to address the problems of "water, compensation for damages resulting from over thirty years of occupation, the environment, future economic relations, and other state-to-state issues."

Abed Rabbo's letter defined itself as "remarks and requests for clarification."[186] Ross described them as "deal-killers."[187] In fact, they were a comprehensive rejection of the Clinton parameters.[188] Abed Rabbo was quoted at the time as saying that "Clinton's proposals are one of the biggest frauds in history, like the Sykes-Picot Agreement."[189]

Arafat arrived in Washington and met with Clinton on 2 January 2001. He reiterated the points made in the letter (which apparently was handed to the Americans only after the Arafat-Clinton meeting) and added new ones. As an example, Clinton recorded that Arafat demanded that several "blocks of the Armenian Quarter" be added to the Old City's Muslim and Christian quarters, earmarked in the parameters for Palestinian sovereignty. Clinton reportedly exploded. "I couldn't believe he was talking to me about this," he understatedly remarked in his memoirs.[190]

The implication of the Palestinian responses to the parameters, as to Barak's proposals from July—and of the way they were later explained by Palestinian spokesmen—was that the PNA-PLO was open to and ready for a two-state settlement, in principle, but that the successive offered packages were inadequate and that Arafat's and Abed Rabbo's "nos" were geared to obtaining better terms rather than expressions of one-state principles. But a close examination of the substance of the "nos" allows for a darker interpretation. The Palestinian insistence on Israel's acceptance of the "right of return" and its implementation, given the demographic realities, would seem to mean that the PNA-PLO strove and is striving for the conversion of Israel from a Jewish to an Arab-majority state as well as a West Bank–Gaza state that is Arab. Presumably these two Arab-majority states would then merge or unify into one Palestinian Arab-majority state. Similarly, Arafat's nonacceptance of shared sovereignty over the Temple Mount implied a basic dismissal of the Jewish claim and right to the mount and, by extension, to Palestine as a whole: the Jews have no recognized historical connection to the Land of Israel and their territorial-political demands are illegitimate. This was Arafat's message at Camp David and has been a constant refrain of Palestinian leaders, from Husseini through Abbas, throughout the history of the Palestinian Arab national movement.

Three weeks later, Israeli and Palestinian teams met for one further bout of negotiation, in Taba, on the Sinai Gulf of 'Aqaba coast. But the talks, held over 21–27 January 2001, were meaningless. Clinton was no longer president, his successor, George W. Bush, had withdrawn support for the parameters, and Barak was facing general elections, on 6 February, that all knew he would lose by a landslide to Ariel Sharon, as in fact occurred. Barak's aides were, politically, in no position to negotiate anything and nothing, in fact, was concluded. Taba was an abortive academic exercise by despondent Israeli doves and powerless Palestinians (Arafat did not attend), no more.

THE SECOND INTIFADA AND THE RISE OF THE HAMAS

The Second Intifada, which had begun at the end of September 2000, tapered off during 2004. It was marked by Palestinian attacks inside Israel as well as in the territories. Most prominent were a succession of suicide bombings by Muslim fundamentalists in Israeli towns, principally against civilian passenger buses and restaurants (suicide bombings, introduced into the region by Hezbollah in the 1980s, were inaugurated by the Palestinian fundamentalists after the Goldstein massacre at the Tomb of the Patriarchs). The Israelis initially responded with air attacks on empty PNA office buildings and police stations, in an effort to prod the PNA into curbing the terrorists, and initiated pinpoint "targeted assassinations," in which individual terrorists and their controllers were killed, usually from the air.

The Israeli strategy failed. Arafat and his aides continued to incite their people to violence. Indeed, the Hamas suicide bombers were soon aped by a growing number of Fatah suicide bombers. The Fatah members were as religious as their Hamas counterparts, and the Fatah leadership feared that the Palestinian masses, enamored with the fundamentalists' "successes," would cross into the Hamas camp. An atmosphere of terror engulfed Israel. In spring 2002 Israel, now under Prime Minister Sharon, struck back. The IDF launched a series of "invasions" or reoccupations of the West Bank's towns, where the bombers made their bombs and from which they ventured forth. Lengthy curfews and economic sanctions were imposed, and there were mass arrests. The Israelis, contrary to Arab and Western press reports, took care, often great care, not to kill civilians. But there were substantial civilian casualties. By 2004, altogether some four thousand Palestinians—about two-thirds of them armed men—and thirteen hundred Israelis—about two-thirds civilians—had died.

The Second Intifada did nothing to push the Palestinians toward accepting a two-state solution. Indeed, because of Israel's countermeasures, the Palestinian rebellion appeared to harden popular attitudes against Israel, which was certainly Hamas's intention in the first place. And the PNA continued to play word games.

Under pressure by the international Quartet—the United States, Russia, the European Union, and the United Nations— to moderate its positions, the Central Committee of the PLO delegated a committee, headed by PNA foreign minister Nabil Sha'at, to draft a Palestinian constitution. On 4 May 2003, the committee issued the so-called 3rd Draft Constitution of the emergent Palestinian state. Its opening Article 1 stated: "Palestine is an independent sovereign state with a republican system. Its territory is an indivisible unit within its borders on the eve of June 4, 1967 and its territorial waters, without prejudice to the rights guaranteed by the international resolutions related to Palestine."[191]

The territorial definition of the Palestinian state is convoluted to the point of obscurity, and it is contradictory. It seems to be saying that the state will be restricted to the West Bank, East Jerusalem, and the Gaza Strip—but it avoids saying so clearly and explicitly. And the second part of the sentence—"without prejudice . . . to Palestine"—implicitly contradicts the vague assurance embedded in the first part because there are countless "international resolutions"—note: it does not say "United Nations resolutions"—that uphold the Palestinian Arabs' claim to all of Palestine. The phrasing allows a great deal of wiggle room.

Moreover, what follows in the draft constitution further subverts the interpretation that the PNA was positing a Palestinian Arab state restricted to the West Bank, Gaza, and East Jerusalem and living alongside Israel in its post-1948 borders. Throughout the document, the drafting committee distinguished clearly between the future "State of Palestine," whose constitution was being drafted, and "Palestine," meaning the land stretching from the Jordan to the Mediterranean. Article 2 states: "Palestine is part of the Arab homeland," and Article 5 states: "Arabic is the official language and Islam is the official religion in Palestine. Christianity and all other monotheistic religions"—how many are there? why not explicitly say "Judaism"?—"are accorded sanctity and respect."

Taken together, these articles to my mind explicitly, and at very least implicitly, provide a firm anchor for anyone asserting that the constitution does not renege on the Palestinians' traditional claim to the whole of Palestine and, in fact, posits a one-state solution. And when capped by Article 7—which states: "The principles of the Islamic Shari'a are the main sources for legislation"—there can be little doubt what sort of state the drafters were envisaging: certainly not a "secular, democratic Palestine."[192]

But whatever the real meaning and intent of the PNC's 1988 "Declaration of Independence"—and this also goes for the 2003 PNA's "Draft Constitution"—it is, in a practical sense, meaningless since there was, and is, no Palestinian Arab state and none has yet come into being. A far more significant document penned the same year as the declaration is "The Covenant of the Islamic Resistance Movement (Hamas)," dated 18 August 1988.[193] It is more significant because from that point on, Hamas steadily gained ground in its struggle for political dominance in Palestine and, in practice, during the Second Intifada overtook Fatah, as was demonstrated in the January 2006 general elections, when it won control of the Palestinian parliament and established a Hamas-dominated government under Prime Minister Ismail Haniyeh. In June 2007 Hamas went on to rout the Fatah-PNA forces in, and physically take over, the Gaza Strip. Since then, it has crushed the remaining Fatah opposition and gradually introduced sharia into that territory. Opinion polls indicate that, in the absence of threatened Israeli intervention, a similar fate awaits the West Bank.

The covenant is Hamas's political constitution and credo. It has never been superseded or annulled; and though recurrently pressured to do so, the Hamas has never amended it or indicated a readiness to change any of its provisions.

The covenant was written by Hamas leaders, headed by the late Sheikh Ahmed Yassin, when the movement emerged like a butterfly from the cocoon of the Palestine branch of the Muslim

Brotherhood, itself an offshoot of the Egyptian parent organization of the same name, during the first months of the First Intifada, which also saw the establishment of Hamas's military wing, the 'Izz al-Din al-Qassam brigades.

Hamas's mindset is deadly serious (I don't remember a Hamas leader ever cracking a joke) and fundamentalist. "The Movement's programme is Islam. From it, it draws its ideas, ways of thinking and understanding the universe, life and man. It resorts to it for judgement in all its conduct, and it is inspired by it for guidance of its footsteps . . . [The Movement] is characterized by its deep understanding, accurate comprehension and complete embrace of all Islamic concepts of all aspects of life, culture, creed, politics, economics, education, society, justice and judgment, the spreading of Islam, education, art, information, science of the occult and conversion to Islam."

When Hamas was founded, the earth was in chaos: "Islam [had] disappeared from life . . . Rules shook, concepts were upset, values changed and evil people took control, oppression and darkness prevailed . . . the state of justice disappeared." It was the role of the Hamas, with "the establishment of the state of Islam," to restore justice to the universe and order to the cosmos, "so that people and things would return each to their right places."

Though Hamas's operations over the years have focused on Israel and the occupied territories, the movement's ideology has potential universal reach or, as the covenant puts it, "its extent in place is anywhere that there are Muslims who embrace Islam as their way of life everywhere in the globe. This being so, it extends to the depth of the earth and reaches out to the heaven . . . the movement is a universal one"—so Americans and Europeans should not be overly surprised if, at some point, Hamas suicide bombers arrive on their doorstep.

But for the present, Hamas's focus is on Israel. "In the name of the Most Merciful Allah," the covenant kicks off, "Israel will exist and will continue to exist until Islam will obliterate it, just as it obliterated others before it"—a reference to the Crusader kingdoms of the Middle Ages.

The covenant defines the ongoing struggle as directed against "the Jews," "they who have received the scriptures," and defines them, in the Qur'an's terminology, as "smitten with vileness wheresoever they are found . . . because they . . . slew the prophets," a reference to the killing of Jesus Christ. The Hamas is deeply, essentially anti-Semitic. "Our struggle against the Jews," states the covenant, "is very great and very serious . . . The Prophet . . . has said: 'The Day of Judgment will not come about until Moslems fight the Jews (killing the Jews), when the Jew will hide behind stones and trees. The stones and trees will say O Moslems, O Abdulla, there is a Jew behind me, come and kill him.'" Citing at one point "The Protocols of the Elders of Zion," the covenant charges that the Jews, "with their money . . . took control of the world media, news agencies, the press, publishing houses, broadcasting stations . . . With their money they stirred revolutions in various parts of the world . . . They were behind the French Revolution, the Communist Revolution and most of the revolutions we heard and hear about . . . With their money they formed secret societies, such as Freemasons, Rotary Clubs, the Lions . . . for the purpose of sabotaging societies and achieving Zionist interests . . . They were behind World War I . . . They were behind World War II, through which they made huge financial gains . . . [It was] they who instigated the replacement of the League of Nations with the United Nations and the Security Council to enable them to rule the world . . . The Zionists aspire to expand from the Nile to the Euphrates . . . [Later] they will aspire to further expansion."

Hamas "strives to raise the banner of Allah over every inch of Palestine," all of which "is an Islamic Waqf [that is, trust] consecrated for future Moslem generations until Judgment Day." In a reference to would-be Arab peacemakers, the covenant asserts that no part of Palestine can be "squandered" or "given up," not by any Arab country or organization, not by "any king or president, nor all the kings and presidents . . . be they Palestinian or Arab." Palestine is forever sacred Islamic soil because, according to "the law governing the land of Palestine in the Islamic Shari'a . . . any land the Moslems have conquered by force . . . during the times of (Islamic) conquests, the Moslems [have] consecrated . . . to Moslem generations till the Day of Judgment." Such lands are inalienably Moslem.

For Hamas, "nationalism . . . is part of the religious creed . . . If other nationalist movements are connected with materialistic, human or regional causes, [the] nationalism of the Islamic Resistance Movement has all these elements as well as the more important [religious] elements that give it soul and life . . . hoisting in the sky of the homeland the heavenly banner that joins earth and heaven with a strong bond."

Hence, the destruction of the Jewish state is Allah's command. And "there is no solution for the Palestinian question except through *jihad*. Initiatives, proposals and international conferences are all a waste of time." Palestine will be reconquered for Islam only through jihad, which all the world's Muslims are enjoined to join. The "liberation of Palestine is . . . the individual duty of every Moslem wherever he may be," "male or female." For Hamas, "Allah is its target, the Prophet is its model, the Koran its constitution: *Jihad* is its path and death for the sake of Allah is the loftiest of its wishes."

Israel is to be destroyed much as the Crusader Kingdom of Jerusalem was destroyed by jihad in the twelfth and thirteenth centuries—and the fate of the Israelis, it is implied, will be much like the Crusaders'. (In the twenty-five-page covenant, the Crusades and Crusaders are mentioned explicitly nine times; the word "jihad" appears eleven times. Saladin, the Kurdish warrior who led the Muslim armies in the destruction of the Kingdom of Jerusalem, is mentioned four times.)

In promoting jihad in Palestine, it is the duty of "scientists, educators and teachers, [and] information and media people" to awaken the masses, to teach "religious duties . . . the Koran . . .

the Prophet's Sunna (his sayings and doings), and . . . Islamic history and heritage from their authentic sources," to "study . . . the enemy," and "to cleanse [the school curriculum] of the traces of [the West's] ideological invasion that affected it as a result of the orientalists and missionaries who infiltrated the region following the defeat of the Crusaders." That infiltration "paved the way for the imperialistic invasion [by General Edmund] Allenby," who commanded the British expeditionary force that defeated the Ottoman Empire in 1917–1918. "All this paved the way towards the loss of Palestine" in 1948.

The covenant defines Hamas's relationship to the PLO in ambiguous terms. On one hand, the PLO "contains the father and the brother, the next of kin and the friend. [And] the Moslem does not estrange himself from his father, brother, next of kin or friend. Our homeland is one . . . our fate is one, and the enemy is a joint enemy to all of us." But "secularism completely contradicts religious ideology . . . That is why . . . without belittling [the PLO's] role . . . we are unable to exchange the present or future Islamic Palestine with the secular idea. The Islamic nature of Palestine is part of our religion."

(The covenant concludes by proclaiming that Hamas "is a humanistic movement. It takes care of human rights and is guided by Islamic tolerance when dealing with the followers of other religions . . . Under the wing of Islam, it is possible for the followers of the three religions—Islam, Christianity and Judaism—to coexist in peace and quiet with each other . . . [But] it is the duty of the followers of other religions to stop disputing the sovereignty of Islam in this region.")

This, then, is the covenant of the leading political party among the Palestinian Arabs, the party that they elected to power in free elections, that thoroughly dominates the Gaza Strip, and that would prevent any other Palestinians, should they so desire, from reaching an accommodation with Israel based on a two-state settlement.

3 Where To?

In the previous chapter I traced the separate trajectories before 1948 of Zionist and Palestinian Arab political thinking about the desired destiny of Palestine. I have shown that both national movements, the Jewish-Zionist national movement from the 1880s and the Palestine Arab national movement from its birth in the 1920s, initially sought sovereignty for their people over the whole country. That was the main political goal of each movement.

But the mainstream of the Zionist movement, led by pragmatic politicians and parties and beset by the Nazi onslaught on European Jewry as well as Arab assault in Palestine, over 1937–1947 gradually pared their goal and acquiesced in the idea of sharing or partitioning the country with the Arabs—not out of altruism or a sense of fairness but because of an appreciation that this was what history was able to offer the Jews, and no more, and because there was an immediate need for Europe's Jews of a safe haven, however small. Thus it was that the Yishuv greeted the UN partition resolution of 29 November 1947 with joy and dancing in the streets. And in the course of the 1948 War, the country was indeed partitioned, with the Jews getting the lion's share (eight thousand square miles), which became the territory of the State of Israel, and the Arabs getting the West Bank and East Jerusalem (under Jordanian control) and the Gaza Strip (under Egyptian control).

During 1949–1967 the majority of Israelis and their successive, Labor-led governments accepted this de facto partition. But the victory in the 1967 Six-Day War and the occupation of the territories awakened among many the desire to constitute a "Greater Israel," encompassing the territory of pre-1967 Israel as well as the newly occupied West Bank, East Jerusalem, and the Gaza Strip (and, perhaps, the Golan Heights and parts of the Sinai Peninsula as well). The incumbent Labor-led government of Levi Eshkol began to establish settlements in the territories, and his successors, Golda Meir and Yitzhak Rabin (and his defense minister, Shimon Peres), modestly continued the policy. The enterprise was then vastly invigorated after the Likud came to power in 1977. Without doubt the establishment, existence, and expansion of the settlements, especially in the hilly heartland of the West Bank, complicated the task of leaders bent on making peace with the Palestinians and reaching a two-state settlement. The Palestinian Arabs did not want Jewish settlements in their "state" after the prospective Israeli withdrawal (though, of course, they saw nothing wrong with the existence of dozens of Arab villages and towns in Israel proper), and the Israeli governments were loath to uproot the settlements or, indeed, curb the settlement enterprise, both because some ministers supported the expansion and out of a reluctance to clash with the settlers and their right-wing supporters. This curtailed the government's ability to advance toward an agreement with the Palestinians.

Be that as it may—and it is clear that the expansion of the settlement enterprise was opposed by much of the Israeli public, and certainly after 1987 by most—the popularity of the Likud-borne expansionist weltanschauung proved short-lived. During the late 1970s and early 1980s the Sinai Peninsula was returned to Egypt in exchange for peace, and following the eruption of the First Intifada in December 1987, the majority of Israelis were persuaded of the desirability of discarding the burden of occupying the heavily Palestinian-populated areas of the West Bank and Gaza Strip. This wish was given electoral expression in the general elections of 1992, when the Likud was voted out of office and Labor rule was reinstituted, with Yitzhak Rabin as prime minister. Thereafter, Israeli politics were, for the most part, dominated by parties—Labor and Kadima—supremely aware of the demographics that were inexorably leading to an Arab majority in a "Greater Israel" and desirous of parting with the Palestinians and the Palestinian territories and reaching a final settlement based on two states. Even the Likud leadership came around to the view that in the long term, ruling over another (and hostile) people was no longer tenable. In 2000, under Labor's Ehud Barak, Israel tried, with American help, to conclude a two-state agreement with Yasser Arafat and the PLO; in summer 2005 Barak's successor, Ariel Sharon, the head of the new Kadima Party, unilaterally uprooted Israel's settlements and pulled the IDF out of the whole of the Gaza Strip, and signaled his intention to do the same, unilaterally, from the bulk of the West Bank as well should the Palestinians prove unwilling to reach a two-state agreement. Israel began to build a barrier—mostly fence, in small parts wall—separating Israel proper from about 93 percent of the West Bank in order to lay the groundwork for a two-state denouement, either through an agreement or, in its absence, unilaterally. This, the demographic imperative, as well as the desire to keep out Arab suicide bombers, was the logic behind the barrier, not discrimination or the desire to steal Arab land (though in delineating the barrier, the planners incorporated in Israel slightly more territory than the Clinton proposals had earmarked for Israel as a cession from the West Bank).

But the possibility of a unilateral Israeli withdrawal from the West Bank was subsequently complicated by the fact that, following the withdrawal from Gaza, the Muslim fundamentalists who dominated the area went on to use it as a launching pad for constant, terroristic rocketing of Israel's border settlements, including the towns of Sderot and Ashqelon (population 120,000).

Israel's leaders quite naturally feared that a similar unilateral pull-back from the West Bank would be followed by a far more dangerous rocketing of the state's main population centers, Jerusalem and the greater Tel Aviv area. It is today clear that no Israeli leader will initiate a pullout from the West Bank—unilaterally or in agreement with the Palestinians—before the IDF acquires the technological capability to protect its population centers from short-range missile attacks. American and Israeli scientists are working on such weaponry, including laser guns, but it is unclear whether such a system will be operational before 2013 and whether it will be effective. Moreover, the countermeasures—laser beams or antirocket missiles—currently being developed are so much more expensive than the costs of producing the primitive Qassam rockets that a protracted attritional contest between the two could impoverish Israel and render the defensive systems ultimately inoperative.

A majority of Israelis still favor a pullback from the West Bank within the framework of a peace agreement with the Palestinians. It is uncertain if such a majority will exist in support of a unilateral pullback. It is also unclear whether most Israelis would support an agreement providing for Israeli withdrawal from all or large parts of Jerusalem; they most certainly will not agree to such a withdrawal without a full, definitive peace settlement. But the overwhelming majority of Israelis, as opinion polls have consistently shown for decades, support partition and a two-state settlement of the conflict. (The results of opinion polls among the Palestinian population, inside and outside Palestine, have been less consistent and more problematic. The nature of the societies and Palestinian politics render the outcomes of such polls less reliable than in Western democracies. Although such polls have often concluded that most Palestinians, at least in the West Bank and Gaza, support a two-state settlement, they have also shown that there is almost complete unanimity among Palestinians in support of the "right of return," the implementation of which would necessarily subvert any two-state settlement. And Palestinian Arabs are equally unanimous in denying the legitimacy of Zionism and Israel—which, again, would raise a vast question mark over the durability of any two-state arrangement.)

Such has been Zionism's political evolution. The evolution of the Palestinian Arab national movement has been radically different. In effect, there has been no evolution in terms of attitudes toward Zionism and Israel. The years 1937, 1947, 1978—when Arafat rejected the Sadat-Begin Camp David Agreements, which provided for Palestinian self-rule in the Gaza Strip and West Bank—and 2000 were all of a piece, with no real movement or change in final objectives. Haj Amin al-Husseini and Arafat were as one in seeking a one-state solution (though a case can be made for asserting that al-Husseini consistently sought Israel's destruction and replacement with a unitary Muslim Arab state in one fell swoop whereas Arafat shuttled between instant one-statism and a phased, staggered approach with the same purpose).

The Palestinian national movement started life with a vision and goal of a Palestinian Muslim Arab-majority state in all of Palestine—a one-state "solution"—and continues to espouse and aim to establish such a state down to the present day. Moreover, and as a corollary, al-Husseini, the Palestinian national leader during the 1930s and 1940s; the PLO, which led the national movement from the 1960s to Arafat's death in November 2004; and Hamas today—all sought and seek to vastly reduce the number of Jewish inhabitants in the country, in other words, to ethnically cleanse Palestine. Al-Husseini and the PLO explicitly declared the aim of limiting Palestinian citizenship to those Jews who had lived in Palestine permanently before 1917 (or, in another version, to limit it to those fifty thousand-odd Jews and their descendants). This goal was spelled out clearly in the Palestinian National Charter and in other documents. Hamas has been publicly more reserved on this issue, but its intentions are clear.

The Palestinian vision was never, as described by various Palestinian spokesmen in the 1960s, 1970s, and 1980s to Western journalists, of a "secular, democratic Palestine" (it certainly sounded more palatable than, say, the "destruction of Israel," which was the goal it was meant to paper over or camouflage). Indeed, "a secular democratic Palestine" had never been the goal of Fatah or the so-called moderate groups that dominated the PLO between the 1960s and the 2006 elections that brought Hamas to power.

Rashid Khalidi has written that "in 1969 [the PLO] amended [its previous goal and henceforward advocated] the establishment of a secular democratic state in Palestine for Muslims, Christians and Jews, replacing Israel."[1] And Ali Abunimah has written, in his recent book, *One Country:* "The PLO did ultimately adopt [in the late 1960s or 1970s] the goal of a secular, democratic state in all Palestine as its official stance."[2]

This is hogwash. The Palestine National Council never amended the Palestine National Charter to the effect that the goal of the PLO was "a secular democratic state in Palestine." The words and notion never figured in the charter or in any PNC or PLO Central Committee or Fatah Executive Committee resolutions, at any time. It is a spin invented for gullible Westerners and was never part of Palestinian mainstream ideology. The Palestinian leadership has never, at any time, endorsed a "secular, democratic Palestine."

The PNC did amend the charter, in 1968 (not 1969). But the thrust of the emendation was to limit non-Arab citizenship in a future Arab-liberated Palestine to "Jews who had normally resided in Palestine until the beginning of the Zionist invasion"—that is, 1917.

True, the amended charter also guaranteed, in the future State of Palestine, "freedom of worship and of visit" to holy sites to all, "without discrimination of race, color, language, or religion." And, no doubt, this was music to liberal Western ears. But it had no connection to the reality or history of contemporary Muslim Arab societies. It was, like all hypocrisy, "a tribute that vice pays to virtue." What Muslim Arab society in the modern age has treated Christians, Jews, pagans, Buddhists, and Hindus with tolerance and as equals? Why should anyone believe that Palestinian Muslim Arabs would behave any differently (vide the departure from Palestinian areas of most Christian Arabs; vide the recent killing of a Christian Arab bookshop owner in Gaza and the torching of the library of Gaza's YMCA)? Western liberals like or pretend to view Palestinian Arabs, indeed all Arabs, as Scandinavians, and refuse to recognize that peoples, for good historical, cultural, and social reasons, are different and behave differently in similar or identical sets of circumstances. (Why, for example, have black Africans, who over the centuries have suffered infinitely more at Western—and, indeed, Muslim Arab—hands than the Arabs ever did, never resort to international terrorism and suicide bombings against Western—or Arab—targets?)

So where did the slogan of "a secular, democratic Palestine" originate? That goal was first explicitly proposed in 1969 by the small Marxist splinter group the Democratic Front for the Liberation of Palestine.[3] According to Khalidi, "It was [then] discreetly but effectively backed by the leaders of the mainstream, dominant Fatah movement . . . The democratic secular state model eventually became the official position of the PLO."[4] As I have said, this is pure invention. The PNC, PLO, and Fatah turned down the DFLP proposal, and it was never adopted or enunciated by any important Palestinian leader or body—though the Western media during the 1970s were forever attributing it to the Palestinians.[5] As a result, however, the myth has taken hold that this was the PLO's official goal through the late 1960s, 1970s, and 1980s.

And today, again, and for the same reasons—the phrase retains its good, multicultural, liberal ring—"a secular, democratic Palestine" is bandied about by Palestinian one-state supporters. And a few one-statists, indeed, may sincerely believe in and desire such a denouement. But given the realities of Palestinian politics and behavior, the phrase objectively serves merely as camouflage for the goal of a Muslim Arab–dominated polity to replace Israel. And, as in the past, the goal of "a secular democratic Palestine" is not the platform or policy of any major Palestinian political institution or party.

Indeed, the idea of a "secular democratic Palestine" is as much a nonstarter today as it was three decades ago. It is a nonstarter primarily because the Palestinian Arabs, like the world's other Muslim Arab communities, are deeply religious and have no respect for democratic values and no tradition of democratic governance. It is indicative that the first major leader of the Palestinian national movement—Haj Amin al-Husseini—was an autocratic cleric who ruled with the gun; and it was no accident that he continuously employed religious symbols and rhetoric to mobilize his people to action against the infidel "invaders." That was the language that could reach the hearts of the Palestinian masses. To have brandished the slogan of a "secular, democratic Palestine" as the national movement's goal, both during the al-Husseini and Arafat years, would simply have alienated the masses—which at least partly explains why the PNC and PLO never adopted it.

And, in this respect, matters have only gotten worse since the 1960s, 1970s, and 1980s. For anyone who has missed the significance of Hamas's electoral victory in 2006 and the violent takeover of the Gaza Strip in 2007, a mere glance at the West Bank and Gaza today (and, indeed, at Israel's Arab minority villages and towns) reveals a landscape dominated by rapidly multiplying mosque minarets, the air filled with the calls to prayer of the muezzins, and alleyways filled with hijab-ed women. Only fools and children were persuaded in 2006–2007 that Hamas beat Fatah merely because they had an uncorrupt image or dispensed aid to the poor. Both were factors, to be sure. But the main reasons for the Hamas victory were religious and political: the growing religiosity of the Palestinian masses and their "recognition" that Hamas embodies the "truth" and, with Allah's help, will lead them to final victory over the infidels, much as the Hamas achieved, through armed struggle, the withdrawal of the infidels from the Gaza Strip in 2005.

In the late 1980s and the 1990s, it appeared as if the PLO, under Yasser Arafat, might be abandoning the one-state goal and adopting a two-state paradigm, envisaging a Palestinian Arab state arising, on 22 percent of historic Mandate Palestine, alongside Israel, and coexisting with it in peace. Such a vision, at least from the Israeli side, underlay the Oslo peace process. But already at the time the sincerity of Arafat's newfound commitment to a two-state settlement was doubtful in view of some of his public pronouncements, his incitement to hatred and terrorism vis-à-vis Israel, and his serial nonimplementation of various provisions, especially those related to curbing terrorism, of the interim agreements he signed during the 1990s. And Arafat was not alone. Various Palestinian bodies and leaders continued through the 1990s to explicitly enunciate the one-state goal. Only under continuous Israeli and American pressure, the PLO very reluctantly appeared to inch away from it. Throughout the period, Arafat, in his speeches in Arabic, persisted in employing terminology—such as "we shall plant the Arab flag on the walls of Jerusalem," "with blood and fire we shall redeem Palestine," and "the sanctity of the Return"—that, for Palestinians, was code for the elimination of Israel and the conquest of all of Palestine. In all, as many Israelis saw it, the Palestinians' prevarication, stonewalling and semantic manipulations in the course of the Oslo process were not so much tactical means to garner the support of a radical public as candid expressions of a will to avoid abandoning the traditional, one-state ideology. Arafat's Johannesburg sermon was both symbol and reality.

Then came the year 2000, with the Barak and Clinton proposals—each better than the last, in terms of the Palestinians—for a two-state settlement, based on the principle, enunciated by Clinton, of two states for two peoples. At Camp David Arafat balked and turned down each successive offer. He refused to compromise on each major core issue—refugees, Jerusalem, Temple Mount, Israeli security, borders—and in December 2000–January 2001 said "no" to Clinton's greatly improved proposals, which offered the Palestinians statehood in 100 percent of the Gaza Strip, 94–96 percent of the West Bank (with some compensation from Israeli territory for the "ceded" areas), and half of Jerusalem.

One possible interpretation of Arafat's stance was that he had simply "overhaggled"; he had wanted better terms and had believed that they were achievable but miscalculated and held out too long, and then was swept up in the violent, radicalizing wash of the Second Intifada, and the chance for a two-state solution, which he genuinely wanted and sought, was lost.

But given his past beliefs and behavior, a more logical interpretation of his behavior in 2000—and, it should be noted, none of his aides (Abu Mazen, Abu Alaa, Nabil Sha'at, Sa'ib Erikat) stood up at the time and dissented from Arafat's "nos"—is that he was still wedded to the one-state solution and wanted all of Palestine. His responses on the Temple Mount issue—"no" to every proposed compromise and his denial of Jewish history and rights—was indicative of his wider mindset: there was no legitimacy to Zionism and Israel or their claims. Arafat rejected the terms offered in July and December 2000 not because of their detail but because of their underlying principle: two states for two peoples.

(Admittedly, this leaves the observer with a problem: if one-state was his endgame, why didn't Arafat simply take what was offered, establish his West Bank–Gaza state, and then tear up the agreement and use that state as a base for "stage 2," the—renewed—assault on and takeover of Israel? Surely this would have made more sense—if Arafat was as duplicitous a leader as I am assuming—than rejecting outright the July–December 2000 proposals and the offered Palestinian state? I have no convincing answer to this except to suggest: one, that Arafat was simply, constitutionally incapable of signing a final, end-of-conflict settlement with "the Jews," and/or two, that he understood that violating in short order such an agreement, with the world looking on and Clinton as witness and guarantor, was simply not an option.)

Arafat and his aides consistently declined to recognize Israel as a "Jewish State," a refusal still characteristic of the PNA leadership. In November 2007, Sa'ib Erikat, the chief Palestinian peace negotiator (and a Palestinian "moderate"), said: "The Palestinians won't accept Israel as a Jewish state."[6] Mahmoud Abbas, the PNA president, put the same idea succinctly a few days later, in Cairo, on his way home from the Annapolis peace summit: "The Palestinians do not accept the formula that the State of Israel is a Jewish State . . . We say that Israel exists and in Israel there are Jews and there are those who are not Jews."[7] So much for two states for two peoples.

Some Palestinian apologists have explained that the PNA was simply bowing to pressure by the Israeli Arab minority leadership, which refuses to recognize Israel as a Jewish state and hopes that one day, through demography and political pressure, Israel will declare itself a non-Jewish state or, as the phrase goes, a "state of all its citizens."

But the problem goes deeper than that. The consistent refusal of the PNA-PLO leadership to accept Israel's Jewishness points to a basic rejection of the two-state approach. Rather, it points to a desire to see the area of Israel eventually revert to an Arab majority presence and rule, whether through war and expulsion, through natural demographic increase among Israel's Arab minority, through a mass refugee return, or a combination of the three. The recent statement to the press by the PNA representative in Lebanon, Abbas Zaki (aka Sharif Mash'al), an old Fatah hand, is exceptional only in its forthrightness, not in its content. "The PLO . . . has not changed its platform even one iota . . . The PLO proceeds through phases . . . Allah willing [we will] drive them out of all of Palestine," he told NBN TV interviewers on 9 April 2008.[8]

Although Abbas, who succeeded Arafat as PNA president in 2005, dresses appropriately and makes many of the right noises vis-à-vis the West (the source of most of the funding that props up the PNA), the sincerity of his two-state avowals remains in doubt, in view of his consistent support for "the right of return" and his refusal to recognize Israel as a "Jewish State." But, in reality, Abbas's true colors are barely relevant. He represents only a small proportion of the Palestinian people. And the absence of popular support and the feebleness of his security forces, as demonstrated during the Hamas takeover of Gaza in June 2007, highlight this irrelevance. In truth, he can deliver nothing. The negotiations he has conducted with Israel since the Annapolis conference in November 2007 can and will lead nowhere; and even if an agreement is reached, a most unlikely prospect, it will be regarded by most Palestinians as a sell-out and will have a short shelf-life and no chance of implementation. Hamas, Islamic Jihad, and the other Palestinian parties and military organizations will continue their war to uproot Israel.

Unfortunately, they, and not Abbas and his bloated, duplicitous apparat ensconced in Ramallah, constitute the real power in the Palestinian territories. And Hamas's policy is laid out in the covenant of 1988 and in the consistent statements of its leadership since then. As Ismail Haniyeh, the Hamas "prime minister," put it at the Gaza rally (attended by 250,000) in December 2007 commemorating the twentieth anniversary of the Hamas's founding, "We will never recognize Israel"—to which the head of Hamas outside Palestine, Khalid Mashal, added, in a video broadcast: "We will never give up one inch of Palestine."[9] Hamas has the virtue of speaking clearly and consistently.

There is an unavoidable logic to the one-state solution. In strictly geographical terms, Palestine/the Land of Israel is indeed "one country." The ("Green") lines established in the Israel-

Jordan and Israel-Egypt armistice agreements of 1949, separating the West Bank and Gaza Strip from the State of Israel, are completely artificial (though the same can be said of the international boundary established in 1923 between Palestine and Lebanon; the Litani River, geographically if not demographically, would have made much more sense). On the other hand, the Jordan River and then the Dead Sea and the 'Arava rift or Wadi 'Araba are a natural boundary between the land lying to the west—Palestine—and Syria and Transjordan (Jordan) in the east.

The division of Palestine into three parts—Israel, the West Bank, and the Gaza Strip—also makes little sense in terms of a variety of resources and services: the country's water resources cannot countenance such an artificial division; the hill-country aquifers in the Galilee-Samaria-Judea highlands necessarily also serve the lowlands below. Nor can a logical sewage system be defined and constructed separately for the West Bank (today, many Palestinian towns and villages, and industries, channel their sewage into the streams that flow downhill, westward, into Israel and the Mediterranean). Haifa and Ashdod are natural ports for the whole of Palestine, and the establishment of a political entity/state in the West Bank without these maritime outlets makes little sense. Indeed, the very shape and smallness of the Land of Israel/Palestine—about fifty miles from east (the Jordan) to west (the Mediterranean)—makes its division into two states a practical nightmare and well nigh unthinkable.

But, over the past century, demography has trumped geography, and the prospect of fashioning one state for the two peoples that inhabit the country is even more illogical and unrealistic than the geopolitical division of the country. In ruling, back in July 1937, against a binational state, the Peel Commission explained: "About 1,000,000 Arabs are in strife, open or latent, with some 400,000 Jews. There is no common ground between them. The Arab community is predominantly Asiatic in character, the Jewish community predominantly European. They differ in religion and in language. Their cultural and social life, their ways of thought and conduct, are as incompatible as their national aspirations."[10] Indeed, both the Zionist and Palestine Arab political leaderships thought and said as much at the time. Moussa Kazim al-Husseini, head of the Palestine Arab Executive, the first leadership body of the Palestine Arab national movement, put it pithily back in 1922: "Nature does not allow the creation of a spirit of cooperation between two peoples so different."[11] And, of course, it was not just a matter of "difference": Arab hatred of the Jews was so profound as to make a common polity an impossibility. As Lord Peel wrote to Colonial Secretary William Ormsby-Gore as he was preparing the royal commission report, "Though I knew there was ill-feeling between Jews and Arabs, I had not realized the depth and intensity of the hatred with which the Jews are held by the Arabs. [And] I did not realize how deep-seated was the Arab fear of Jewish overlordship and domination."[12]

Nothing has changed since 1937. Or, more accurately, things have changed mainly in directions that make the establishment of a viable binational state even less likely than seventy years ago. During the intervening decades, the fear and hatred of the "other" in each community have grown considerably—as a result, on the Jewish side, of the bouts of Arab terrorism, which have progressively increased in viciousness and scope, and the growing Islamization and political radicalization of the Palestinian Arabs; and, on the Arab side, as a result of their violent defeat, displacement, and dispossession in 1948, the subsequent bouts of Israeli counterterrorist operations that have often resulted in substantial civilian death, and the grinding, stifling Israeli occupation of the territories that has contributed substantially to the psychological, political, and economic misery of the inhabitants since 1967. If Arab expressions in the early years of the twentieth century of fear of eventual displacement and expulsion by the Zionists were largely propagandistic, today—in view of what has happened—they are very real. And if Jewish fears in the 1930s of Arab intentions to push them "into the sea"—to destroy the Zionist enterprise and perhaps slaughter the Yishuv—were, if heartfelt, unrealistic (as it turned out), today they are very real, as are Jewish fears of a nuclear Holocaust at Islamic hands. These fears and hatreds make a shared binational state, in which each community inevitably would seek to dominate the other, if only to prevent the other's domination of itself, inconceivable.

In *The One-State Solution*, Virginia Tilley writes at length about Arab hatred of Israel and the Jews, in the end dismissing it as marginal and ephemeral. In effect, she denies Jewish assertions that the Arabs hate the Jews/Israel and pooh-poohs the argument that, in a one-state situation, the Arabs would "quickly doom Jewish Israelis to marginalization, oppression, and even expulsion. The Arabs, it is believed, have always sworn to 'throw the Jews into the sea' and will do so at the first opportunity. Israel's remaining a Jewish state. . . . is therefore argued as an imperative against persistent Arab and Muslim hostility."[13]

Tilley argues, on the contrary, that "although Arabs are certainly not immune from anti-Semitism, Arab language against 'the Jews'" is a response primarily to the explicit Zionist "privileging of 'the Jews' and to the Palestinians' expulsion and dispossession." No, Arabs do not really hate the Jews, she writes. For example, take the suicide bombers, who for more than a decade now have haunted Israel's buses and restaurants: "Relative to the scope of the military occupation and the size of the Palestinian population under occupation, suicide bombings and other attacks—despite their broadly terrifying impact—have remained a tiny fringe phenomenon," she writes.[14] But Tilley ignores the broad popularity that these suicide bombings enjoyed—and still enjoy—in the Palestinian cities, ignores the crowds that swamped the streets of Ramallah and Gaza and Nablus when news arrived of a "success" in Tel Aviv or Haifa; ignores the Fatah/Hamas custom of handing out sweets to passersby with each "successful" bombing; and ignores the veneration the bombers are accorded in all West Bank and Gaza schools, their postered faces looking down from the walls in every classroom. Second, the relatively small number of successful suicide bombings during the years 1993–2008 was a function more of Shin Bet and IDF prevention and interdiction (and the security fence) than of Palestinian inhibitions or restraint. The suicide bombings, as every poll among Palestinians has shown, were, and remain, immensely popular.

Tilley goes on: "The mass behavior of nearly 2.5 million [sic] Palestinians under occupation . . . indicates that the vast majority of Palestinians remain impressively resistant to outright racial hatred. The enemy is Israel and Zionism, not Judaism per se. 'The Jews' are feared and detested because they incarnate the occupation policy that oppresses Palestinians." Tilley adds that, "although Arab and Palestinian rhetoric certainly called for expelling Jewish settlers from Palestinian land, they never seriously suggested their physical annihilation on anything like the racial terms of National Socialism."[15] She compares Palestine/Israel to what happened in Algeria in the 1960s and says that the Arab societies in both deemed settler colonization "illegitimate"—but she fails to note that in the Algerian case, the Arabs ended up driving out the country's million-odd white settlers, lock, stock, and barrel.

Ignoring the ample evidence provided by Hamas, Tilley discounts charges of Arab Judeophobia or anti-Semitism. Of course, there is anti-Semitism in all communities, she concedes, but evidence of Arab anti-Semitic racism is so thin that Zionist accusations "commonly must center on just one genuinely racist figure: the incompetent and reactionary Grand Mufti of Jerusalem, Haj Amin al-Husseini." But, she maintains, he "was never a leader of more than a few reactionary Palestinian factions. His primary accomplishment was to sideline and obscure for history those Arab factions that sought coexistence with the Jewish-Zionist movement. (Not to excuse al-Husseini but to contextualize him, we also might recall that various Zionists, including the Haganah, also attempted ineffectually to collaborate with Hitler in the 1930s, on the opposite agenda . . .)."[16]

The sheer quantity of untruths in this passage is striking, even by Tilley-land standards: al-Husseini was the head of Palestine's Supreme Muslim Council between 1922 and 1948 and the head of the Arab Higher Committee during 1936–1939 and again in 1946–1948, and, during the 1930s and 1940s, he was recognized by both the Arab masses of Palestine and the neighboring Arab governments, as well as by the British Mandate government and by the Jewish authorities in Palestine, as the leader of the Palestinian national movement. No Palestinian historian or commentator disputes this. To claim now that he represented merely "a few reactionary Palestinian factions" is plain mendacity. Second, there were no "Arab factions" "that sought coexistence with the Jewish-Zionist movement." No Arab party during the 1930s and 1940s sought coexistence; all sought to crush the Yishuv and rule all of Palestine themselves, though a minority may occasionally have temporized or sought tactical, short-term accommodations. Last, the Haganah, to the best of my knowledge, never sought "to collaborate" with the Nazis in the 1930s. There was one extremist Zionist paramilitary or terrorist group, the LHI, or "Stern Gang," with some three hundred to five hundred members (the Haganah at this time had twenty thousand to thirty thousand members) and no popular backing—in the 1949 Knesset elections the LHI veterans party won no seats—which sought an alliance with the Germans, during 1939–1940, before the Holocaust got under way, in order to jointly fight against and throw out of Palestine what they regarded as the British "imperialists." The Nazis, of course, refused to have anything to do with them.

Last, Tilley argues: "In any case, the flamboyant rhetoric used by Arab leaderships in the 1960s to encourage expelling 'the Jews' is long gone; it had not been heard in any public forum for twenty years, until, ominously, it was whipped up among extremist Islamic sectors by the U.S. occupation of Iraq in 2003."[17] Now although it is true that the PLO leadership since the 1960s has learned the arts of verbal restraint and ambiguity, Tilley apparently has never heard of Hamas, which continues to exercise far fewer inhibitions of this sort (though, it is true, its leadership does refrain from using explicit phrases like "throwing the Jews into the sea"). Nonetheless, to charge Washington with responsibility for recent Palestinian expulsionist thinking, as embodied in the Hamas covenant and the Fatah constitution, is a rank absurdity. Tilley may not like America's war in Iraq. But neither of these documents was inspired by anything that happened in or was done by the United States.

But to return to demography. Regarding the potential for a binational solution, matters have changed for the worse since the 1930s in other ways. As the Muslim proportion of the Palestine Arab population has grown, and grown more devout, so the proportion of Christians—the more Westernized and "liberal" sector among the Arabs—has steadily diminished (it now stands at less than 5 percent); Christian Arab families have tended to have fewer children and, proportionately, have emigrated in far greater numbers to the West and out of the conflict.

At the same time, the massive immigration of Jews from Islamic lands to Israel in the late 1940s, 1950s and 1960s has increased the Sephardi proportion of the Jewish population. This has had a double effect. On one hand, the country's Jewish community to a degree has been orientalized, for example, in cuisine and various aspects of public behavior. This might have helped pave the way to binationalism (via some shared values—the centrality of family and clan, for example—among Israeli Sephardis, at least of the first, immigrating generation, with the Palestine Arabs). But these "orientalizing" factors have been offset by the psychological and ideological baggage these immigrants brought with them and which they passed down to their children and grandchildren—which contained an essential hatred for the Arabs, stemming from the discrimination and occasional violence they had suffered in the Muslim-majority countries from whence they came, and commensurate hard-line, anti-Arab politics and voting patterns once in Israel. At the same time, the second, third, and fourth generations of Sephardi descent have gradually been Westernized, distancing them, in terms of values, from the Arab societies of their familial origin. Today, most Israeli Jews, both Ashkenazi and Sephardi, look to the West for their values, ideas, markets, holidays, books, movies, music, and television shows.

A second demographic change on the Jewish side, speeded up by the events of 1967, was the vast increase in the proportion of ultra-Orthodox and Orthodox Jews in the overall population and the decline in the proportion of secular Jews, who are generally more liberal and open-minded than their religious compatriots. This change has been reflected in the steady growth of ultra-Orthodox and Orthodox political representation and power in both Labor- and Likud-led coalition governments. (For example, in Jerusalem, Israel's most populous city at 650,000 inhabitants, the demographic changes have resulted in the election for the first time, in 2003, of an ultra-Orthodox mayor with an ultra-Orthodox–Orthodox majority in the municipal council.) The Orthodox and ultra-Orthodox are generally hard-liners on Arab-related issues and prone to expansionist and racist thinking.

The large, one-million-strong wave of immigrants who arrived in Israel from the Soviet Union and its former component republics in the late 1980s and 1990s, with the collapse of communism, injected a large, secular population into the Jewish demographic tableau. But this has not appreciably aided the cause of binationalism. The Soviet *olim* tended to bring with them hard-line, right-wing political instincts. Among the Russian Jews in Israel there will be few takers for the binational paradigm; they and their parents endured anti-Semitism and saw quite enough of life among, alongside, and under the Gentiles. For them, the Arabs are just a new version of Gentiles—and ones for whom they generally have contempt.

Despite some of the foregoing, Israeli Jewish society remains largely secular, with Western, democratic values predominating. These can hardly dovetail with the authoritarian and religious values of Palestine Arab society, which is moving steadily toward greater religiosity. Forty years ago few Arab women in the territories and inside Israel wore scarves or veils; today they are the norm. Decades ago, there were functioning cinema houses in the Gaza Strip and the West Bank (and East Jerusalem); today there are none. The second-class status of women and the ostracism, indeed vilification, of homosexuals are norms in West Bank and Gaza society (as in most of the Arab world), and honor killings, both in Israeli Arab society and in the Palestinian territories—of wives, sisters, daughters—for infringing traditional behavioral or dress codes or for flirting with the wrong males, let alone for sleeping with them, are common. These are not the norms of Israeli Jewish society. And Hamas, an anti-democratic organization, demonstrated in the June 2007 takeover of the Gaza Strip that it has no respect for what are accepted in the West as civilized values—they shot captured Fatah men in the knees and then threw them off of tall buildings—and will discard even their semblance, as a snake sheds its skin, the moment they prove inconvenient.

The mindset and basic values of Israeli Jewish society and Palestinian Muslim society are so different and mutually exclusive as to render a vision of binational statehood tenable only in the most disconnected and unrealistic of minds. The value placed on human life and the rule of (secular) law is completely different—as exhibited, in Israel itself, in the vast hiatus between Jewish and Arab perpetration of crimes[18] and lethal road traffic violations.[19] Arabs, to put it simply, proportionally commit far more crimes (and not only ones connected to property) and commit far more lethal traffic violations than do Jews. In large measure, this is a function of different value systems (such as the respect accorded to human life and the rule of law). And to these contrasting value systems must be added the different, often conflictual, collective memories and histories of the two societies, their different languages and cultures, and the large economic and educational gap that separates them. Each of these alone would probably constitute an insuperable barrier to successful binationalism. (Look at contemporary Belgium, which seems to be heading for partition over little more than language.)

And, of course, there are the political-ideological obstacles. On the Jewish side, there is an insurmountable basic problem: Zionism set out to solve the Jewish problem by establishing a

Jewish polity, inhabited and governed largely if not solely by Jews, a place where Jews could, at long last, not live as a minority in someone else's house, by his leave. And Zionism achieved this in 1948: a Jewish-majority state. Sixty years on, Israel's Jews overwhelmingly still want this—and refuse to share sovereignty in their state with another people, and certainly will fiercely resist any attempt to turn them into a minority in what they regard as their own land. And most Israeli Jews believe that this would be the end-result of the establishment of a binational state, given greater Arab birthrates and the potential mass return of Palestinian refugees.

But from the Arab side, the rejectionism is at least equally comprehensive and deeply felt. The idea of sharing Palestine (as indeed, the sharing of any Muslim Arab land with non-Muslims and non-Arabs)—either through a division of the country into two states, one Jewish, the other Arab, or through a unitary binational entity, based on political parity between the two communities—is alien to the Muslim Arab mindset. Since the seventh and eighth centuries, when the Hijazi tribes swept out of Arabia and conquered the (largely Christian) Middle East and North Africa as far west as southern France, Muslim Arabs have been dominant, by law and by force, in their social and political environment, even when, as in the early years of the Islamic surge, the Muslim Arabs were in a minority. And, following the conquest of non-Arab areas, the Muslim Arabs have, in the long run, sought to attain a majority, through forced conversion, slaughter, and/or expulsion. From the eighth or ninth centuries, Muslim Arabs have been politically dominant in the Islamic world and have grown accustomed to that position; the notion of sharing power or being a minority in a non-Muslim Arab polity is alien to the Muslim Arab mentality. In the Muslim Arab world there have never been binational or bireligious political structures. There are only polities where Muslim Arabs are masters or, when in a minority, where they aspire to attain majority and mastery.

But if, for the reasons enumerated, a binational state, with political parity for the two communities, is not realistic, what about other possible one-state solutions? There are four possible variants: a Jewish state encompassing the whole of Palestine, without any Arabs; an Arab state encompassing the whole of Palestine, without any Jews; a Jewish-majority state, with a substantial Arab minority; and an Arab-majority state, with a substantial Jewish majority.

The first two appear at the moment to be wholly unrealistic. A Jewish state without an Arab minority would require the murder or expulsion of the 4–4.8 million Arabs (1.3 million Israeli Arabs, 2 million Arab inhabitants of the West Bank, and 1–1.5 million inhabitants of the Gaza Strip) living in the country, or some combination of the two. Israeli Jewish society is incapable, for moral and political reasons, of murdering millions or hundreds of thousands of Arabs. It is also inconceivable that Palestine's

Arab inhabitants would abandon the country of their own free will. But a campaign of expulsion, as required to rid the country of all or most of its Arab population, would doubtless take weeks if not months to implement and would be halted in its tracks by the international community and by much of Israel's Jewish public.

Similarly, the achievement of a Jew-less Land of Israel through murder or expulsion or a combination of the two by the Arabs would in all likelihood be stymied by the international community, or at least the United States, which might well intervene militarily. Given Arab actions, and inaction, regarding recent events in Darfur or, during earlier decades, regarding similar events in southern Sudan, Yemen, and Syria, among other places, it is doubtful whether Palestinian Arab society or Arab societies around Palestine would have inhibitions about destroying Israel's Jews or at least standing aside and allowing others to carry out such destruction. But Western intervention, or fear of Western intervention, would most likely inhibit such mass murder, so the destruction or expulsion of the country's millions of Jews is, at present, inconceivable.[20] And of course, it is extremely unlikely that Israel's Jews would leave the country and go into exile of their own free will (especially since most of them would not readily find host countries to resettle in).

Which leaves us with the remaining two variants, of a Jewish majority state, with a substantial Arab minority, and an Arab-majority state, with a substantial Jewish minority. The Peel Commission, back in 1937, addressed both possibilities. It ruled that it would be unjust to establish either an Arab-majority state in all of Palestine, in which the Arabs would dominate the Jews, or a Jewish-majority state in all of Palestine, in which Jews would lord it over the Arabs. Neither arrangement would result in peace. Rather the opposite; the resulting situation would be of endless instability, with rebellions, irredentism, and foreign interventions the order of the day.

The Peel Commission had no historical precedent to go by in looking at the nature of a possible one-state solution with a Jewish majority and an Arab minority. There had never been such a polity. But, to be sure, the commissioners understood that the Arabs of Palestine, and perhaps those of the surrounding states, would never acquiesce in such an arrangement and that it would be a recipe for perpetual violence and warfare, whether or not the Jews treated the Arab minority fairly.

But the commission certainly had plenty of historical precedents for the opposite arrangement, of states with Arab Muslim majorities and Jewish minorities. And the history of such states gave no grounds for optimism about the possible fair treatment of the minority by the majority. Indeed, Islamic history was replete with empires and states controlled by Arab Muslim majorities with Jewish (and other) minorities—and the minorities had always been discriminated against, often oppressed and persecuted, expelled and repeatedly slaughtered, or subjected to forced conversions (contrary to what Arab propagandists, eager for a one-state, Muslim majority–Jewish minority solution in Palestine, are wont to tell gullible audiences in the West). That is why the Arab Middle East and North Africa, which were Christian-majority areas before the Islamic conquests, now have almost no Christian or Jewish populations (the sole exceptions being Egypt, with its cowed Coptic Christian minority, and Sudan, with its embattled Christian communities in the south, which over the decades have suffered more than a million deaths at Muslim hands).

Jews and Christians in all the Islamic lands paid discriminatory taxes and were always regarded and treated as second-class citizens; and Jews, being powerless, were always regarded with contempt. Although in most places at most times Jews were protected by the Muslim ruler of the day, they were recurrently persecuted and subjected to pogroms, especially in the peripheries of Muslim empires and in times of internal crisis or turmoil. Even in areas, such as Spain, where Jews attained prominence in society, the arts, and even politics, pogroms occurred (for example, nearly three thousand were slaughtered in Granada in 1066; and in the twelfth century, under the Almohads, almost all the Jews in Andalusia were forcibly converted to Islam or expelled). Elsewhere, pogroms were more frequent and deadly. In Fez, Morocco, some six thousand were slaughtered in 1033, and many others died in the city in pogroms in 1276, 1465, and 1912. In Baghdad there were periodic pogroms; in the most recent, in June 1941, Muslim mobs murdered between one hundred and three hundred Jews, and hundreds of Jewish-owned shops and houses were torched.

To be sure, the rise of Zionism and events in Palestine in the first half of the twentieth century reinforced the traditional Arab animosity toward the Jews and, in 1947–1948, resulted in a series of pogroms against assorted Jewish communities (in Aden, Syria, Bahrain, and Morocco) as well as state-organized extortion of "fines" and mass incarcerations (in Iraq and Egypt).[21] The Peel Commission was aware of the earlier historical record and opposed consigning the Jews in Palestine to Muslim-majority rule.

A similar appreciation of the past and of the prospective future underlies the resistance of Israeli Jews to the notion of transforming the territory of Israel and the West Bank and Gaza into a unitary Palestinian polity in which they would be, or would shortly become, a minority in a Muslim Arab-majority state. Indeed, should such a unitary state ever emerge, its Jews, or as many of them as could, would, in all likelihood, emigrate to the West, leaving behind only the ultra-Orthodox, bound to the land out of deep religious conviction, and those incapable of finding new homes elsewhere. Most Israeli Jews without doubt would prefer life as a minority in the West, where they would enjoy that world's openness and freedoms, to the stifling darkness, intolerance, authoritarianism, and insularity of the Arab world and its treatment of minority populations.

So, if a one-state solution is a nonstarter, what are the prospects for a two-state solution? Put simply, they appear very bleak. Bleak primarily because the Palestinian Arabs, in the deepest fibers of their being, oppose such an outcome, demanding, as they did since the dawn of their national movement, all of Palestine as their patrimony. And I would hazard that, in the highly unlikely event that Israel and the PNA were in the coming years to sign a two-state agreement, it would in short order unravel. It would be subverted and overthrown by those forces in the Palestinian camp—probably representing Palestinian Arab majority opinion and certainly representing the historic will of the Palestinian national movement—bent on having all of Palestine. To judge from its past behavior, the PNA would be unwilling and, probably, incapable of reining in the more militant, expansionist factions—Hamas, Islamic Jihad, and so on—who would represent themselves as carrying on the patriotic, religious duty of resisting the Zionist invader. No Palestinian leader can fight them without being dubbed a "traitor" and losing his public's support. Without doubt, the Israeli settlements in the West Bank have increased Palestinian militancy and motivation to fight Zionism and add a further layer of obstruction to any possibility of partitioning the land into two viable states—though the example and precedent of Israel's uprooting of all its settlements from the Gaza Strip in 2005 indicates that the majority of West Bank settlements, too, could be removed should the Israeli government and public come to believe that such a course would assure Israel peace and future prosperity. But given Palestinian behavior and discourse—and this must include the observation that the Israeli pullout from the Gaza Strip did nothing to moderate Palestinian behavior and attitudes toward Israel; rather the opposite—there is little chance that Israelis will come to feel and believe this in the foreseeable future.

Beyond this, there are good objective reasons why a two-state solution of the sort proposed by Ehud Barak and Bill Clinton back in 2000 can have little traction even among Palestinians who, in principle, might agree to such a compromise. The division of historic Mandatory Palestine as proposed, of 79 percent for the Jews and 21 percent for the Palestinian Arabs, cannot fail to leave the Arabs, all Arabs, with a deep sense of injustice, affront, and humiliation and a legitimate perception that a state consisting of the Gaza Strip and the West Bank (and perhaps large parts of East Jerusalem)—altogether some two thousand square miles—is simply not viable, politically and economically. It cannot begin to stand on its own two feet economically and certainly cannot solve the problem posed by millions of Palestinian refugees bent on repatriation. Indeed, it is doubtful whether such a small state could meet the needs of its own refugee and nonrefugee populations. Many of Gaza's impoverished families would doubtless try to resettle in the more spacious West Bank. The West Bank's own refugee communities would demand rehabilitation and orderly resettlement within the territory. How much of the West Bank, if any, would be left over for absorbing the refugee communities from Lebanon and Syria—some eight hundred thousand souls, stateless and largely impoverished—is anyone's guess. And there are large numbers of refugees in Jordan as well who might seek to move to the Palestinian state.

Such a West Bank–Gaza state, therefore, driven by objective economic, demographic, and political factors, would inevitably seek more territory and would try to expand. Most likely, Israel, for sound ideological and geographic reasons, would be the target of preference for such expansion—though the Palestinian state would probably also seek to incorporate Jordan, where some 70 percent of the population is of Palestinian origin (refugees from 1948 and 1967 and their descendants) as well. The Egyptians might also feel a similar expansionist thrust from the Gaza Strip toward El Arish in Sinai. Such Palestinian expansionism would leave the region in perpetual turmoil.

So a two-state settlement along the lines proposed by Barak and Clinton in 2000 is unlikely to come about or, if reached, to last long. It will not bring tranquility to the Middle East. And yet the two-state idea—the idea of a state for the Jews and a state for the Palestinian Arabs—remains the only sound moral and political basis for a solution offering a modicum of justice and, hence, a chance for peace, for both peoples.

One possible avenue for a two-state solution that might conceivably mobilize wide Arab public support lies by way of a large Middle Eastern federation or confederation of states in which a small Jewish state would be but a part. This, at least, was a view held by prominent British and Zionist officials, and some Arab politicians, during the late 1930s and early 1940s.

The "ideological" basis for such a settlement was the conviction that the region's Arabs might find a Jewish state more palatable within the framework of a large confederation or federation than if it were established straightforwardly over all of Palestine or in part of a partitioned Palestine. As historian Yehoshua Porath formulated it, the "basic assumptions" were "that the inclusion of Palestine in a broader Arab framework would alleviate, in part at least, some of the fears [of Jewish demographic or economic dominance] that the Palestine Arabs felt as a result of the growth of the Jewish settlement in Palestine, and that a political fulfillment of the unity goal of Arab nationalism would counterbalance the partial loss of Arab national rights in Palestine."[22]

The idea apparently was first proposed by Britain's first high commissioner in Palestine, Herbert Samuel, in 1920. He suggested that the confederation be ruled from Damascus. During the mid-1930s, David Ben-Gurion, then chairman of the Jewish Agency Executive, sounded out a variety of Palestinian Arab notables, including Musa al-'Alami and George Antonius, on the idea. Judah Leib Magnes, too, raised the federal or confederal idea as a framework that could accommodate the binational polity he favored.[23]

The idea of an Arab federation or confederation won favor during the dying days of World War II among British and

American officials keen on containing Soviet expansionism in the Middle East; this, from the British side, was the driving force behind their promotion of the "League of Arab States" (the Arab League) that emerged in 1944–1945.[24] But by then it was not the need to find an acceptable Arab framework for an emergent Jewish state that was powering the idea.

The federal or confederal idea, of a vast Arab polity with a small Jewish political component, was in fact a nonstarter for one simple reason: the Arabs abhorred the idea of a Jewish political entity in the Middle East, however camouflaged or softened by an Arab regional framework. Moreover, the envisaged framework was to be Arab. A Jewish state in its midst, indeed, at its heart, whatever its envisioned benefits for the Arabs, would have been unnatural in the extreme.

But a trace of the idea has descended down the decades to our time in the form of a narrower confederation, putatively composed of Israel, the West Bank and Gaza, and Jordan. Perhaps the establishment of such a confederation would solve the prospective unviability of the West Bank–Gaza Palestinian state and the problematics of an East Bank Jordanian state cut off from the Mediterranean and composed largely of a Palestinian population. As with the plans from the 1930s and 1940s, this confederal idea might help sell the idea of the Jewish state to the region's Arabs, while economically and geopolitically, such a confederation offers a viability lacking for each of its separate parts.

But certainly since the outbreak of the First Intifada in 1987, such confederal thinking has been brushed aside by the thrust and violence of the Palestinian pursuit of a more delimited and focused self-determination. Yet the prospect of a Palestinian state composed of the Gaza Strip and the bulk of the West Bank, as perhaps sincerely envisaged by President George W. Bush and Prime Minister Ehud Olmert, brings us back to questions of viability and sufficiency and the expected Palestinian expansionism of a state that would be unable to accommodate the Palestinian refugee Diaspora. And the idea of Palestinians and Israelis, after 120 years of warfare, convivially sharing power even in a confederal framework is probably unacceptable to most Jewish Israelis and most Palestinian Arabs at this point in their histories.

Yet one, still narrower confederal or federal idea remains standing. Which brings me back to the Israeli Labor Party concept from the 1970s and 1980s, never officially adopted by the party but accepted by most of its leaders, of a partition of Palestine into Israel, more or less along its pre-1967 borders, and an Arab state, call it Palestinian-Jordanian, that fuses the bulk of the West Bank and East Jerusalem and the east bank, the present-day Kingdom of Jordan. For such a newfangled state to emerge and succeed, the government, in Amman (or East Jerusalem?), would necessarily need to be a cooperative enterprise of the Hashemite regime, based on the core bedouin population of Jordan, and the PNA, based on the Palestinian populations of the West Bank, the Gaza Strip, and Jordan. Given the relative size (thirty-seven thousand square miles) and emptiness of Jordan, such a state would allow for the redistribution of the Palestinian population of overcrowded Gaza and the absorption of the bulk of the refugees currently living in statelessness in Lebanon and Syria, as well as, given sufficient capital, enabling the orderly resettlement of Jordan's vast refugee population, much of it living in dismal refugee "suburbs" around Amman. Such a fusion of the Palestinian territories and Jordan would blunt the edge of Palestinian expansionist needs and motivations, though most likely it would still face the opposition of the fundamentalists bent on Israel's overthrow and conquest and the imposition of sharia over all of Palestine and, indeed, the Middle East. But the unification of the PNA and Jordan, with its relatively powerful army and security services, would provide the possibility of reining in the militants (much as Jordan has easily and successfully reined in its own Palestinian and Islamist militants over the past decades).

To be sure, the emergence of a joint West Bank–Gaza–Jordan state, ruled jointly by the Hashemites and the PNA, would most likely incur opposition from the Hashemites and their Jordanian bedouin constituency, who until now have ruled Jordan without real power sharing with the country's majority Palestinian population. Indeed, the Hashemites might well fear that the fusion of the Palestinian territories with Jordan would lead to Palestinian empowerment, ending, eventually, in their own ouster. Such fears would need to be addressed and neutralized in the constitution of the joint Palestinian-Jordanian state.

In the 1970s and 1980s, in light of Israeli political inability or unwillingness to give back the West Bank, and the mindsets, policies, and pressures of the Arab world and the PLO, Jordan, under King Hussein, gave up the idea of winning back the West Bank, or its bulk, through talks with Israel and reintegrating it within the Hashemite kingdom. But the inability of the Israelis and Palestinians since then to reach an agreement and bring forth a West Bank–Gaza Palestinian state must give all concerned pause to reconsider Jordan's divorce from the West Bank and open the door to Israeli-PNA-Jordanian negotiations geared to reaching such a two-state settlement. Such negotiations would no doubt encounter violent opposition from Islamic fundamentalist countries and factions and, perhaps, various other Palestinian groups. But given current realities, this would seem the only logical—and possible—way forward.

Notes

Chapter 1. The Reemergence of One-Statism

1. Over the past few years, against the backdrop of the Second Intifada and Israel's efforts to suppress Arab terrorism, Palestinian spokespeople have stepped up their designation of Israel's policies as "apartheid." Without doubt, the definition "sells" well in the West and serves the Palestinian goal of delegitimizing Israel much as South Africa's apartheid regime was delegitimized in the West before its collapse. But Israeli journalist Sever Plutzker (in "Who Favors a Partition Plan?" Y-Net, 3 January 2008) has pointed out that these years have also witnessed a gradual replacement, among Palestinian spokesmen, of "the discourse of occupation" with the "discourse of apartheid" because the focus on berating the "occupation" leads, or should lead, to Israeli withdrawal from the territories, opening the way for a two-state solution, whereas the talk of "apartheid," with its stress on human rights and their absence, should lead, eventually, to ameliorating the situation of the oppressed within the existing geopolitical framework. Plutzker

points out that this shift of emphasis corresponds to the shift among Palestinians from advocacy of a two-state solution to advocacy of one-statism; talking of "apartheid" serves the "one-state" purpose.

2. Khalidi, *Iron Cage*, 206–210.

3. Sofer, "Israel, Demography, 2000–2020," 18.

4. Bistrov and Sofer, *Israel, 2007–2020*.

5. According to the United Nations, there are more than four million Palestinian refugees: just two million live in the West Bank and Gaza Strip; the rest live mainly in Lebanon, Syria, and Jordan. By "refugees" is meant those who were displaced during the 1948 War and are still living and their descendants. According to the PLO, there are five to six million refugees. Almost to a person, Palestinian intellectuals and spokespeople, left, right, secular, and fundamentalist, support the refugees' "right of return" to their homes and lands in pre-1967 Israel. For example, the independent Anglo-Palestinian researcher Salman Abu Sitta has argued since the 1990s that a one-state solution is necessary and possible and that the Palestinian refugees should and can easily return to the area that became the State of Israel in 1948–1949. His chief argument is that "78 per cent of the Jews live in 14 per cent of Israel" (Abu Sitta, "Right of Return," 199)—hence, the four to six million refugees could "simply" return to the 86 percent of historic Palestine that is either inhabited by Israeli Arabs or is uninhabited. For example, "All the refugees in Lebanon should return to the Galilee and all the refugees in Gaza should return to Beersheba. It is simple. The number . . . in Lebanon . . . is . . . 399,000, and those of Gaza . . . [is] 700,000. If we return them, the Jewish areas will not be affected at all" (*Akhbar al Naqab*, 6 December 1998).

6. Tilley, *One-State*, 234, 184.

7. Abunimah, *One Country*, 16.

8. Abunimah, *One Country*, 7.

9. Abunimah, *One Country*, 66.

10. Abunimah, *One Country*, 192.
11. Morris, *Road to Jerusalem*, 90–104.
12. Morris, *1948*, 375–391.

Chapter 2. The History of One-State and Two-State Solutions

1. I thank Dr. Amikam Elad for help with some of these definitions, though the textual upshot is mine alone.
2. See al-Khalidi to Khan, 1 March 1899, in Be'eri, *Beginning*, 89–90; and Mandel, *Arabs and Zionism*, 47–48.
3. Sakakini, *Such Am I, Oh World*, entry for 31 March 1936, 184.
4. Vital, *Origins of Zionism*, 368, emphasis added.
5. Shapira, *Land and Power*, 55.
6. Ben-Yehuda to Peretz Smolenskin, July 1882, in Be'eri, *Beginning*, 38.
7. Herzl, *Diaries*, entry for 3 September 1897, 2:581.
8. Ben-Yehuda and Yehiel Michal Pines to Rashi Pin, October 1882, in Be'eri, *Beginning*, 38–39, emphasis in original.
9. Azoury, *Le reveil*, 6–7. Azoury seems to have believed that the Zionists wished to take over not just Palestine but all the lands between the Nile and the Euphrates, in line with biblical prophecy. Arab spokesmen, in their effort to brand Zionism as expansionist, were later frequently to repeat this.
10. "Statement of the Zionist Organisation Regarding Palestine," 3 February 1919, PRO FO 371-4170.
11. Biger, *Land of Many Boundaries*, 161–163.
12. Weizmann to Churchill, 1 March 1921, in Weizmann, *Letters*, 10:160.
13. Weizmann to Churchill, 19 September 1919, in Weizmann, *Letters*, 9:221. Weizmann had enclosed with his letter Aaronsohn's "Memorandum on the Boundaries of Palestine."
14. Ben-Gurion and Ben-Zvi, *Land of Israel in Past and Present*, 45–46.
15. Weizmann to Churchill, 1 March 1921, in Weizmann, *Letters*, 10: 160–161.

16. Naor, *Greater Israel*, 76.

17. Naor, *Greater Israel*, 76–77.

18. Heller, *Brit Shalom*, 11.

19. Ruppin, *Memoirs*, entry for 26 April 1925, 217.

20. Ruppin, *Memoirs*, entry for 18 November 1925, 220.

21. 14 August 1925, quoted in Hattis, *Bi-National Idea*, 44–45.

22. Heller, *Brit Shalom*, 11.

23. "Memorandum by the Brit Shalom Society on the Arab Policy of the Jewish Agency," January 1930, in Hattis, *Bi-National Idea*, 51–52.

24. Simon, "Memorandum," 12 March 1930, in Hattis, *Bi-National Idea*, 54.

25. Hattis, *Bi-National Idea*, 57, quoting Ruppin to Victor Jacobson, 3 December 1931, 203.

26. Ruppin, *Memoirs*, entry for 17 October 1929, 248.

27. Ruppin, *Memoirs*, entry for 25 April 1936, 277.

28. Hattis, *Bi-National Idea*, 162–163.

29. Heller, *Brit Shalom*, 203.

30. Heller, *Brit Shalom*, 202.

31. Heller, *Brit Shalom*, 204, n. 4.

32. Buber, 26 December 1942, quoted in Heller, *Brit Shalom*, 244.

33. Heller, *Brit Shalom*, 250.

34. Magnes to Weizmann, 7 September 1929, in Goren, *Dissenter in Zion*, 276.

35. Magnes to Weizmann, 25 May 1913, in Goren, *Dissenter in Zion*, 137.

36. Magnes at the convocation of the Hebrew University academic year, autumn 1929, quoted in Goren, *Dissenter in Zion*, 34–35.

37. Magnes to Felix Warburg, 13 September 1929, in Goren, *Dissenter in Zion*, 279.

38. Magnes to "Friend" (possibly Norman Bentwich), May 1920, in Goren, *Dissenter in Zion*, 183–190.

39. Magnes in 1929, quoted in Goren, *Dissenter in Zion*, 34–35.

40. Magnes, address in Jerusalem, 22 May 1922, in Goren, *Dissenter in Zion*, 213.

41. Magnes, Journal, "Brit Shalom," 14 September 1928, in Goren, *Dissenter in Zion*, 272–273.

42. Magnes, statement in *New York Times*, 24 November 1929, in Goren, *Dissenter in Zion*, 282–285. To this Weizmann retorted that the "Jews want [a] homeland not [a] cultural museum" (see Goren, *Dissenter in Zion*, 205).

43. Magnes, "Note," 29 October 1932, in Goren, *Dissenter in Zion*, 294.

44. Magnes, "Journal: Shabbat Veyehi," 18 December 1937, in Goren, *Dissenter in Zion*, 338.

45. Note by [unknown], "The Christians," PRO CO 733 347/10.

46. Price, "Periodical Appreciation Summary No. 11/36," 23 June 1936, PRO FO 371-20018.

47. Cohen, *Army of Shadows*, 97.

48. Cohen, *Army of Shadows*, 109.

49. Cohen, *Army of Shadows*, 111.

50. Cohen, *Army of Shadows*, 140.

51. Magnes to Ben-Gurion, 3 March 1938, in Goren, *Dissenter in Zion*, 349–350.

52. Magnes, "Towards Peace in Palestine," 392.

53. Magnes, "Notes: Conversation with Azzam Pasha, Cairo," 18 May 1946, in Goren, *Dissenter in Zion*, 433.

54. Magnes, "Report on Arrival in the United States," New York, 26 April 1948, in Goren, *Dissenter in Zion*, 485.

55. Zayit, *Pioneers*, 25.

56. Hattis, *Bi-National Idea*, 71.

57. "Resolutions, the Sixth General Council (Mishmar Ha'emek, 10–17 April 1942)," HHA 5.20.3 (2). The resolutions explicitly distinguished between an "Arab federation" spawned by "imperialist intrigues or the Arab reaction" and a federation resulting from the development, if it occurred, of "the Arab national movement, so that it becomes an expression of the aspiration for social liberation of the laboring masses."

58. Hattis, *Bi-National Idea*, 72.

59. Hattis, *Bi-National Idea*, 85.

60. Weizmann to James Marshall, 17 January 1930, *Letters and Papers of Weizmann*, 14: 207.

61. Hattis, *Bi-National Idea*, 91.

62. Hattis, *Bi-National Idea*, 223.

63. Hattis, *Bi-National Idea*, 251.

64. Hattis, *Bi-National Idea*, 122.

65. Storrs, *Orientations*, 447. Earlier, in April 1936, Archer Cust published the idea in "Cantonisation: A Plan for Palestine," *Journal of the Royal Asian Society*, xxiii.

66. *Palestine Royal Commission Report*, 379.

67. Magnes, "Telegram to Appear in *New York Times*," 18 July 1937, PRO FO 371-20810.

68. One senior Foreign Office official, George Rendel, commented on the report and the idea of a small Jewish state: "The State will be far too small, its frontiers will be far too artificial, and it will be subjected to far too many servitudes, ever to be able successfully to stand alone in what are described in the Covenant of the League [of Nations] as the 'strenuous conditions of the modern world.' Indeed, although the Jews might spend vast sums on armaments and dispose of all the most modern engines of warfare, I find it hard to believe that such a small and artificial province, of a highly civilised and industrialised character, clinging, as it were, onto the edge of the Arab world, will possess any real elements of stability, if it is to be constituted into an entirely independent international unit. The days of such tiny States in exposed positions are past; and it must be remembered that the whole Arab and Eastern world may very easily adopt the attitude that the Jewish State which has been forced by Europe onto an unwilling Arabia, must one day be destroyed. We can no longer rely on the East never changing, and it

may be that in a measurable space of time the Middle Eastern Moslem countries will after all become efficient and organised and prove a formidable danger to this little Jewish territory" (Rendel, "Palestine: Future of Proposed Jewish State," 1 July 1937, PRO FO 371-20808).

69. R[eginald] C[oupland], "Note for Discussion of Partition," undated, PRO CO 733 346/9.

70. D. Ben-Gurion to Amos Ben-Gurion, 5 October 1937, Ben-Gurion Correspondence, IDFA.

71. Herzl, *Complete Diaries*, entry for 12 June 1895, 1:88. There are academics who contend that Herzl's reference here was to a Jewish state to be established in South America rather than in Palestine (see HaCohen and Kimmerling "Note on Herzl"; see also Morris, "Comment on HaCohen and Kimmerling").

72. Masalha, *Expulsion*, 11–12, 37.

73. Kisch to Weizmann, 20 May 1930, quoted in Morris, *Birth of Palestinian Problem Revisited*, 44.

74. As Yitzhak Avigdor Wilkansky, a prominent Zionist agronomist, put it in December 1918: "If it were possible [to evict Arab peasants], I would commit an injustice towards the Arabs. There are those among us who are opposed to this from the point of view of supreme righteousness and morality . . . [But] we must be either complete vegetarians or meat-eaters; not one-half, one-third or one-quarter vegetarians" (quoted in Caplan, *Palestine Jewry*, 29).

75. *Palestine Royal Commission Report*, 391.

76. D. Ben-Gurion to A. Ben-Gurion, 27–28 July 1937, Ben-Gurion Correspondence, IDFA.

77. Protocol of meeting of 7 August 1937, CZA S25-1543.

78. Protocol of the joint meeting of the Jewish Agency Executive and the Political Committee of the Zionist Actions Committee, 12 June 1938, CZA S100-24b.

79. "Short Minutes of Meeting Held on Thursday, January 30th, 1941, at 77 Great Russell Street, London, W.C.1.," Chaim Weizmann Archive, 2271.

80. "Note on Conversation with General Nuri Sa'id, the Iraqi Prime Minister and the Iraqi Minister of Foreign Affairs in Baghdad on 5th and 6th December 1944," 18 December 1944, PRO FO 921-149; Alec Kirkbride to Thomas Wikeley, FO, 29 July 1946, PRO FO 816/85, and Kirkbride to FO, 23 August 1946 (nos. 1387, 1364), both in PRO FO 816/85.

81. Morris, *Birth of Palestinian Problem Revisited*, 39–40. The UN-defined Jewish state, with 550,000 Jews, was to have had an Arab minority of 400,000–490,000.

82. Naor, *Greater Israel*, 90.

83. Naor, *Greater Israel*, 105.

84. Naor, *Greater Israel*, 106–111.

85. Katz, *Jabo*, 2:1000–1002.

86. Naor, *Greater Israel*, 86–87.

87. Naor, *Greater Israel*, 87.

88. Eldad, *State of Israel*, 7; Naor, *Greater Israel*, 102.

89. Magnes, "Address to the Council of the Jewish Agency," Zurich, 18 August 1937, in Goren, *Dissenter in Zion*, 331.

90. Gelber, *Jewish-Transjordanian Relations*, 205.

91. Morris, *Road to Jerusalem*, 91–117.

92. Magnes, letter to the editor, *New York Times*, 28 September 1947, in Goren, *Dissenter in Zion*, 451–456.

93. Naor, *Greater Israel*, 91.

94. Naor, *Greater Israel*, 93.

95. Naor, *Greater Israel*, 94–95.

96. "Ben-Gurion's Announcement," *Haaretz*, 30 November 1947.

97. Israel cabinet meeting protocol, 26 September 1948, ISA.

98. Allon to Ben-Gurion, 27 March 1949, BGA Correspondence.

99. Quoted in Naor, *Greater Israel*, 9.

100. Quoted in Naor, *Greater Israel*. 61.

101. Naor, *Greater Israel*, 35.

102. Some revisionist Israeli historians (see Meital, "Khartoum Conference") will have us believe that that explicit pan-Arab "no" actually meant "yes." They are not very persuasive.

103. Gorenberg, *Accidental Empire*, 42–120.

104. Gorenberg, *Accidental Empire*, 59–61.

105. Naor, *Greater Israel*, 66.

106. Naor, *Greater Israel*, 92.

107. Shlaim, *Lion of Jordan*, 292. See Shlaim, *Lion of Jordan*, 192–201, 220–222, 259–264, 288–296, 335–337, 361–364, 381–383, etc., for descriptions of Hussein's meeting with the various Israeli leaders.

108. Porath, *Emergence of Palestinian Arab National Movement*, 109; Hattis, *Bi-National Idea*, 36; Muslih, *Origins of Palestinian Nationalism*, 207–208.

109. Palestine Arab Delegation to Colonial Secretary, 21 February 1922, CZA S25-7678.

110. Moussa Kazim el-Husseini, president of the Palestine Arab Delegation, and Shibly Jamal, secretary, to Colonial Secretary, 17 June 1922, CZA S25-7678.

111. Hattis, *Bi-National Idea*, 19–20.

112. Hattis, *Bi-National Idea*, 64.

113. Central Archives for the History of the Jewish People, Jerusalem, P3-2436. Ben-Gurion, to whom Magnes sent a copy of Khalidi's proposal, commented: "The proposal is interesting as it comes from an Arab. To me it seems that from an *Arab* standpoint it is undesirable as it leaves them with only the poor hill country and gives them no outlet to the sea" (Ben-Gurion to Magnes, undated, in same file).

114. Khalidi to Magnes, 23 July 1934, P3-2436.

115. Hattis, *Bi-National Idea*, 126.

116. Hattis, *Bi-National Idea*, 196, quoting Bentwich to Arthur Louria, 22 July 1937.

117. Cohen, *Palestine and the Great Powers*, 141–147, 197–202.

118. Heller, *Brit Shalom*, 258–264.

119. Heller, *Brit Shalom*, 318–327.

120. Hattis, *Bi-National Idea*, 292.

121. Quoted in Hattis, *Bi-National Idea*, 314–315.

122. Porath, *Riots to Rebellion*, 231.

123. "Iraqi Prime Minister's Disapproval," *Times* (London), 14 July 1937.

124. "Arab Delegations," *Haaretz*, 12 July 1937; "Iraqi Antipathy to Partition," *Times* (London), 16 July 1937.

125. "Palestine Still Critical," *Times*, 10 July 1937.

126. "Partition of Palestine: A Tour through the North," *Times*, 14 July 1937.

127. Nashashibi, *Jerusalem's Other Voice*, 151, quoting *Manchester Guardian* interview, 2 December 1937.

128. [Signature illegible], Government House, Jerusalem, to Arthur Wauchope, 17 November 1937, PRO CO 733 354/1.

129. "Information of the Arab Bureau," "From Oved," 3 June 1937, which tells of two local National Defense Party rallies, at Sheikh Muwannis and "in a village near Jenin," "supporting the Emir [Abdullah] and the idea of partition," CZA S25-3575.

130. Porath, *Riots to Rebellion*, 229; Nashashibi, *Jerusalem's Other Voice*, 96.

131. "The Nashashibis Too Are Against Partition," *Haaretz*, 12 July 1937. Nashashibi, *Jerusalem's Other Voice*, misrepresents the Opposition's stance when he writes simply: "Ragheb and the National Defense Party were alone in informing the British High Commissioner of their acceptance of the report" (101).

132. Nashashibi to High Commissioner, 21 July 1937, PRO FO 371-20810 ("The Partition scheme does not only undermine the national

existence of the Arab people, [it] shatters their unity and threatens the Arabs with immediate dispersion and extermination"). See also Porath, *Riots to Rebellion*, 229.

133. Nashashibi, *Jerusalem's Other Voice*, 65.

134. Nashashibi, *Jerusalem's Other Voice*, 131.

135. Nashashibi, *Jerusalem's Other Voice*, 91–92.

136. Cohen, *Army of Shadows*, 145–147.

137. Antonius, *Arab Awakening*, 408–409, 412.

138. Antonius, *Arab Awakening*, 408, 410.

139. Antonius, *Arab Awakening*, 411.

140. Antonius, *Arab Awakening*, 411–412. During the last years of the Mandate there were a handful of Arabs who supported partition. But their number and significance were risible. Most were driven by a desire for revenge. The most prominent was 'Omar Sidqi al-Dajani, from a notable Jerusalem family, whose father had been murdered by al-Husseini gunmen during the revolt. He subsequently served as a Haganah Intelligence Service agent, codenamed by the HIS "*hayatom*" (the orphan) (Gelber, *Budding Fleur-de-Lis*, 110, 229, etc.; Cohen, *Army of Shadows*, 238).

141. Elpeleg, *In the Eyes of the Mufti*, 148–149.

142. Quoted in Wasserstein, *British in Palestine*, 41.

143. *Palestine Royal Commission Report*, 141. Elsewhere, more explicitly, Peel wrote, in passing, of "the Arab proposal to banish the Jews [of Palestine]" (see Peel to Ormsby-Gore, 20 December 1936, PRO CO 733 297/5).

144. Ben-Gurion, *Meetings with Arab Leaders*, 197.

145. Heller, *Brit Shalom*, 344.

146. Quoted in Shemesh, "Crisis," 2:342. At the time of the British conquest there were slightly fewer than sixty thousand Jews in Palestine.

147. Nadia Lourie, "Interview with Mrs. Mogannam [Mughannam]," 10 January 1948, CZA S25-9005.

148. Ibn Sa'ud to Truman, 26 October 1947, *FRUS*, 1947, 5:1212–1213.

149. Khalidi, *Iron Cage*, 190.

150. Sayigh, *Armed Struggle*, 87–88.

151. Sayigh, *Armed Struggle*, 212.

152. http://www.ipcri.org/files/fatah1964.html. The constitution lays out the "penalties" for violating its provisions as: "drawing attention, rebuke, warning, freezing, rank demotion, firing, firing with slander." The "violations" include "violating the Movement political line, violating the freedom of expression rule, disrespect of leading authorities' decisions, disrespect of hierarchy, offending the public, offending other members, offending reputation, [spreading] false rumours."

153. Sayigh, *Armed Struggle*, 212.

154. Sayigh, *Armed Struggle*, 212–213.

155. Sayigh, *Armed Struggle*, 250.

156. Sayigh, *Armed Struggle*, 334–335, quoting from Hassan, *Genius of Failure*, 128–129, 144.

157. "Political Program Adopted at the 12th Session of the Palestine National Council, Cairo, 8 June 1974," at http://www.un.int/palestine/PLO/docone.html.

158. Gresh, *PLO*, 159.

159. Gresh, *PLO*, 159–160.

160. Khalidi, *Iron Cage*, 154.

161. Gresh, *PLO*, 179, wrote that the PNC resolutions were "a turning point in Palestinian political thought." See also Tessler, *History of the Israeli-Palestinian Conflict*, 481–499. Khalidi, *Iron Cage*, 153–154, comments: "It may have been the case that the exaggerated expectations about the PLO on the part of outsiders were rooted in sympathy for the Palestinian people, in the general positive aura that once surrounded national liberation movements, and especially in approval of the PLO's revised goal of a Palestinian state alongside Israel."

162. Sayigh, *Armed Struggle*, 343.

163. "Agenda Item 108," Arafat's speech at the UN General Assembly, 13 November 1974, at http://domino.un.org/UNISPAL.NSF/ db942872b9eae45485256of6005a76fb/a238ec7a3e1.

164. "Declaration by the Palestinian National Council in Cairo (March 22, 1977)," at http://www.jewishvirtuallibrary.org/jsource/Peace/ pncdeclare.html.

165. Sayigh, *Armed Struggle*, 417.

166. Tessler, *History of the Israeli-Palestinian Conflict*, 536.

167. *Middle East Mirror*, 2 June 1988; Peretz, *Intifada*, 112, 185.

168. Shalev, *Intifada*, 153–154; Schiff and Ya'ari, *Intifada*, 283–284.

169. "Palestinian Declaration of Independence, November 15th, 1988," in http://www.mideastweb.org/plc1988.htm.

170. Khalidi, *Iron Cage*, 195.

171. The texts of Arafat to Rabin, 9 September 1993, and Rabin to Arafat, 10 September 1993, as well as of the DOP, are in Government of Israel, Ministry of Foreign Affairs, September 1993, "Declaration of Principles on Interim Self-Government Arrangements," 38–39.

172. Full text of "Arafat's Speech in Johannesburg 10 May 1994," at http://www.textfiles.com/politics/arafat.txt. There are scholars who maintain that Muhammad was not the first to violate the truce.

173. Quoted from *Al-Arab*, 22 April 2004, in "Palestine Liberation Organisation," at http://www.indopedia.org/Palestine_Liberation_Organization.html.

174. "Letter from President Yasser Arafat to President Clinton," posted 13 January 1998, at http://www.miftah.org/Display.cfm?DocId=428&CategoryId=10.

175. "Remarks by President Clinton to the Palestinian National Council and other Palestinian Organizations, Shawwa Center, Gaza, 14 December 1998," at www.mtholyoke.edu/acad/intrel/clintplo.htm.

176. Clinton, *My Life*, 911–916; Sher, *Beyond Reach*, 153–235; Ben-'Ami, *Front without a Rearguard*, 129–232; Ross, *Missing Peace*, 650–711. It

is noteworthy that no senior Palestinian participant has published an equivalent, detailed record of what happened at Camp David, day by day, blow by blow. Perhaps this is due to the calculation that, if the account was dishonest, it would immediately be exposed; and if it was honest, it would in the main reinforce the version published by the Israelis and Americans—thus raising a large question mark about why Arafat rejected what was on offer.

177. Ross, at the beginning of *Missing Peace*, in unnumbered pages, offers the reader maps (1) ". . . Reflecting Actual Proposal at [End of] Camp David" and (2) "Palestinian Characterization of the Final Proposal at Camp David." Ross's maps are reproduced at the front of this book. They show that Arafat was offered a contiguous 91 percent of the West Bank, without a sovereign Israeli strip from Ma'ale Adumin to the Jordan River bisecting it. These maps give the lie to Palestinian charges, after Camp David, that they had been offered only disconnected "cantons" or "bantustans," an argument that they thereafter used to justify their rejection of the Barak-Clinton offers and the launching of the Second Intifada.

178. Ross, *Missing Peace*, 705.

179. Clinton, *My Life*, 915.

180. Ross, *Missing Peace*, 694; Enderlin, *Shattered Dreams*, 257–259.

181. "The Clinton Parameters . . . Meeting with President Clinton, White House, December 23 2000," at http://www.peacelobby.org/clinton_parameters.htm; Ross, *Missing Peace*, 801–805.

182. See "Bomb Blast Rocks Israel," http://news.bbc.co.uk/1/hi/world/middle_east/1090670.stm.

183. Sher to Sandy Berger, 5 January 2001, and "Points of Clarification," personal archive. This is the first publication of the main points of this document. Interestingly, in dealing with refugees, the "Points of Clarification" also stated: "Israel assumes that the issue of Jewish refugees [i.e., from Arab countries, referring to the hundreds of thou-

sands of Jews intimidated into flight from Yemen, Egypt, Syria, Iraq, etc., during the post-1948 years] would also be addressed." On security issues, the "Points" "assumed" that the "multinational force" would be "US-led", would "guarantee" "the non-militarization of Palestine [i.e., the future Palestinian state] through the deployment along its aerial, land and maritime perimeter including at all entry points" and that there would be "Israeli control" of operational airspace over Palestine and "the electromagnetic spectrum of Palestine." Moreover, "no other armed forces [i.e., of other states] . . . could be stationed or deployed in, or pass through or over Palestinian territories."

184. Clinton, *My Life*, 938; Ross, *Missing Peace*, 755.

185. The Palestinians seem to have had a valid point with respect to the exclusion of the northwestern quadrant of the Dead Sea, no-man's-land, and the greater Jerusalem area from the calculation of the West Bank percentages. They were probably also right about the disadvantageous ratio of the territorial compensation for the ceded West Bank areas—but no one had ever promised them a one-to-one ratio. And they were definitely wrong in alleging that the area Israel proposed to cede was a "toxic waste" dump. No area had been specified by Clinton or the Israelis.

186. "Official Palestinian Response to the Clinton Parameters (and letter to International Community)," 1 January 2001, at http://www.robat .scl.net/content/NAD/negotiations/clinton_clinton_parameters/para m2.php.

187. Ross, *Missing Peace*, 756. Ross said that they involved "rejection of the Western Wall part of the formula on the Haram . . . rejection of the most basic elements of the Israeli security needs, and . . . dismissal of our refugee formula."

188. Palestinian spokesmen and Arab apologists during the following weeks and years were to claim alternatively (1) that Arafat had not said

"no" to the proposals and (2) that both Israel and Arafat equally had said "no." Mearsheimer and Walt, in *Israel Lobby*, 107, for example, argue that "the official Palestinian response . . . asked for clarification on some points, and expressed reservations about others . . . Thus both the Palestinians and the Israelis accepted the Clinton Parameters and saw them as the basis for continued negotiation, but neither side accepted them in toto." This evenhandedness is, at core, mendacious, and dovetails with the duo's many other dishonesties.

189. Morris, *Righteous Victims*, 671. It is unclear what he meant as there was nothing "fraudulent" about the secret Anglo-French 1916 Sykes-Picot Agreement—though, to be sure, it was condemned by the Arabs once they discovered its terms. The agreement carved out future zones of direct and indirect British and French control in the Arab-speaking areas between modern-day Turkey and Saudi Arabia.

190. Clinton, *My Life*, 943. Clinton commented that Arafat appeared "confused" and "not . . . at the top of his game."

191. See http://www.pcpsr.org/domestic/2003/nbrowne.pdf for text of the 3rd Draft Constitution and comments by Prof. Nathan Brown. Brown, a political scientist at George Washington University, who translated the document into English and published it, under the auspices of the Palestinian Center for Policy and Survey Research, based in Ramallah, commented on this: "The implications of this clause are clear: The state of Palestine lays claim to all of the West Bank (including East Jerusalem) and Gaza but to no other territory . . . This is (to my knowledge) the first authoritative document . . . detailing the specific territorial boundaries of that state."

192. In the commentary that Brown appends to each clause, he argues that "the principles of the Islamic Shari'a" are not tantamount to "Shari'a." This is not very persuasive. Incidentally, in the constitutions of almost all the Muslim Arab states, shari'a is defined as the basis of the state's laws.

193. "Hamas Covenant 1988," at http://www.yale.edu/lawweb/avalon/ mideast/hamas.html. All that follows is quoted from "The Avalon Project at Yale [University] Law School" translation of the covenant.

Chapter 3. Where To?

1. Khalidi, *Iron Cage*, 154.

2. Abunimah, *One Country*, 108. His book is suffused with liberal blather unconnected to Middle Eastern realities but geared to massaging British sensibilities. The book demonstrates that Abunimah knows neither the Palestinians nor the Israelis, nor the history of their conflict.

3. Karmi, "Secular Democratic State." Karmi—more accurately than Khalidi and Abunimah—writes that in 1969 the PNC adopted a "modified version" of the goal, calling for a "democratic state of Palestine." But Karmi adds that the idea "was quietly dropped after 1974."

4. Khalidi, *Iron Cage*, 191–192.

5. See, e.g., *Time*, 25 November 1974, in its essay on Arafat's speech at the UN General Assembly, "Guns and Olive Branches." *Time* stated that the PLO leader's objective was "to create a new secular democratic state of Palestine." But Arafat had said no such thing.

6. See "Israeli-Palestinian Team Hold 'Difficult' Talks," 12 November 2007, in http://www.reuters.com/article/latestCrisis/idUSL127 112048.

7. Abbas to reporters, Cairo, 1 December 2007, Jewish Telegraphic Agency report, 2 December 2007.

8. http://www.memritv.org/clip/en/1738.htm.

9. Avi Issacharoff, "Mashal in the Rally Commemorating Twenty Years to the Hamas: We Have Strength for Two More Intifadas," and Issacharoff and Amos Harel, "The Unity Remained in the Words," both in *Haaretz*, 16 December 2007. Wishful thinkers and naïfs like

Henry Siegman ("Israel: The Threat from Within," *New York Review of Books*, 26 February 2004) might periodically "discover" "a change of policy" by the Hamas leadership. But it is all illusion. The Hamas leaders, from Ahmed Yassin onward, have been nothing if not consistent. They have, on occasion, proposed temporary truces, *hudna*s, with Israel, usually appending conditions such as Israeli withdrawal to the 1967 borders or Israel's acceptance of the "right of return." And they have intermittently agreed to limited ceasefires, or *tahadiya*s (one was agreed, through Egyptian mediation, between the two sides in June 2008), aimed at winning brief respites or advantages. But these overtures have always been tactical. On the strategic, goal-related plane, Hamas has been unwavering: no recognition of Israel, no peace, and the eventual restoration of Islamic Arab rule in every inch of Palestine.

10. *Peel Commission Report*, 370.

11. Moussa Kazim al-Husseini, president of the Palestine Arab Delegation, and Shibly Jamal, Secretary, to Colonial Secretary, 17 June 1922, CZA S25-7678.

12. Peel to Ormsby-Gore, 20 December 1936, PRO CO 733 297/5.

13. Tilley, *One-State*, 161–162.

14. Tilley, *One-State*, 162–163.

15. Tilley, *One-State*, 163–164.

16. Tilley, *One-State*, 164–165

17. Tilley, *One-State*, 165. Even allowing for the inevitability of bias, it is beyond me how a book containing such nonsense can be taken seriously. Yet Tony Judt's back-cover blurb calls it "clear," "trenchant" and "courageous," as performing "a signal scholarly and political function."

18. Arabs, proportionately, commit between three and ten times as many crimes as Jews, according to Israel Police statistics. With Israel's Arabs representing 16–18 percent of Israel's citizenry (Druze are a separate category and are not treated here), 16,755 files (investigations) were opened in 2002 by police against Israeli Arab citizens for violations of

public order (bribery, threats, illegal gambling, trespassing, etc.), and 5,401 persons were convicted. That year, 27,861 police files were opened against Jews for identical offenses and 7,374 were convicted. That year, police opened 678 files against Israeli Arabs for offenses against persons (including murder, attempted murder, manslaughter, etc.); 405 were convicted. Among Jews, the figures were 233 and 107, respectively. That same year, 429 files for sex offenses (rape, attempted rape, etc.) were opened against Arabs; 141 were convicted (and, presumably, many Arab sex offenses were committed within their own communities, where publication and the involvement of police are generally considered taboo); among Jews, the figures for that year were 1,932 and 554, respectively. That year 9,293 files were opened against Israeli Arabs for crimes against property (theft, robbery, etc.); 3,434 were convicted. For the Jews, the respective statistics were 22,396 and 7,827.

The proportions remained much the same through the decade. In 2007, 24,852 files were opened against Arabs for crimes against public order; 2,216 were convicted. For Jews, the respective statistics that year were 35,032 and 1,862. That year 334 files were opened against Jews for crimes against people (murder, etc.); 14 were convicted. The figures for Arabs were 666 and 63 respectively. That year, files were opened against 556 Arabs for sex crimes; 37 were convicted. For Jews, the respective figures that year were 2,127 and 56. That year 10,792 files were opened against Arabs for crimes against property; 1,203 were convicted. For Jews, the respective figures were 17,741 and 1,246. In some categories of serious crime, more Arabs than Jews or as many Arabs as Jews were investigated by police and/or convicted—though Arabs represented roughly one sixth of Israel's population (Chief Inspector Hamutal Sabagh to the author, 27 May 2008, and appended Internal Security and Police Ministry statistics for 2002–2007, in my possession).

19. Internal Security Minister Avi Dichter on 27 December 2007 noted that Israeli Arabs were responsible, per capita, for twice as many road deaths as Jews (Kol Israel, 27 December 2007).

20. Because this book is limited to dealing with the Israelis and Palestinians (and, less directly, the wider the Arab world), I will not relate to the possibility of a future Israeli-Iranian conflict and to one of its more horrific, possible permutations, once Iran acquires nuclear weaponry—namely, Israel's destruction with these weapons.

21. Morris, *Birth of Palestinian Problem Revisited*, 412–416.

22. Porath, *Arab Unity*, 58.

23. Porath, *Arab Unity*, 58–148.

24. Porath, *Arab Unity*, 257–311.

Bibliography

Archives

Central Zionist Archive (CZA), Jerusalem

David Ben-Gurion Archive (BGA), Sdeh Boqer

Israel Defense Forces Archive (IDFA), Tel Hashomer

Israel State Archive (ISA), Jerusalem

Public Record Office (PRO), London

Chaim Weizmann Archive, Rehovot

Periodicals

Haaretz

London Review of Books

New York Review of Books

New York Times

Time

The Times (London)

Bibliography

Published Documents

US State Department. *Foreign Relations of the United States* (FRUS), 1947, vol. 5.

Palestine Royal Commission (Peel Commission) Report. London: HMSO, 1937, cmd. 5479.

Books and Articles

Abunimah, Ali. *One Country: A Bold Proposal to End the Israeli-Palestinian Impasse*. New York: Metropolitan Books, Henry Holt, 2006.

Abu Sitta, Salman. "The Right of Return: Sacred, Legal and Possible." In Naseer Aruri, ed., *Palestinian Refugees: The Right of Return*, 195–207. London: Pluto Books, 2001.

Antonius, George. *The Arab Awakening: The Story of the Arab National Movement*. New York: Capricorn Books, 1965.

Aruri, Naseer, ed. *Palestinian Refugees: The Right of Return*. London: Pluto Press, 2001.

Azoury, Negib. *Le reveil de la nation Arabe dans l'Asie turque*. Paris: Plon, 1905.

Barghouti, Omar. "Relative Humanity: The Fundamental Obstacle to a One-State Solution in Historic Palestine." http://www.dissentvoice.org, 13 January 2004.

Bartov, Omer. Letter to the editor. *New York Review of Books*, 4 December 2003.

Be'eri, Eliezer. [Hebrew.] *The Beginning of the Israeli-Arab Conflict*. Tel Aviv: Sifriyat Poalim/Haifa University, Institute for the Study of the Middle East, 1985.

Ben-Ami, Shlomo. [Hebrew.] *A Front without a Rearguard*. Tel Aviv: Yediot Aharonot, 2004.

Ben-Gurion, David, and Yitzhak Ben-Zvi. [Hebrew.] *The Land of Israel in the Past and Present*. Jerusalem: Yad Yitzhak Ben-Zvi, 1980 [orig. publ. in Yiddish, New York, 1918].

Ben-Gurion, David. [Hebrew.] *My Meetings with Arab Leaders.* Tel Aviv: Am Oved/Keren Hanegev, 1975.

Biger, Gideon. [Hebrew.] *Land of Many Boundaries: The First Hundred Years of Demarcating the Borders of the Land of Israel, 1840–1947.* Beersheba: Center for the Heritage of Ben-Gurion, Sdeh Boqer/Ben-Gurion University Press, 2001.

Bistrov, Yevgenia, and Arnon Sofer. *Israel, 2007–2020: On Demography and Over-Population.* Haikin Chair for Geostrategy, Haifa University, December 2007.

Caplan, Neil. *Palestine Jewry and the Palestine Question, 1917–1925.* London: Frank Cass, 1978.

Clinton, Bill. *My Life.* New York: Alfred A. Knopf, 2004.

Cohen, Hillel. *Army of Shadows: Palestinian Collaboration with Zionism, 1917–1948.* Berkeley: University of California Press, 2008.

Cohen, Michael. *Palestine and the Great Powers, 1945–1948.* Princeton, NJ: Princeton University Press, 1982.

Eilon, Amos. Letter to the editor. *New York Review of Books,* 4 December 2003.

Eldad, Yisrael. [Hebrew.] *The State of Israel: A Bridgehead to the Kingdom of Israel.* Jerusalem: Sulam, 1960.

Elpeleg, Zvi. [Hebrew.] *In the Eyes of the Mufti: The Essays of Haj Amin Translated and Annotated.* Tel Aviv: Moshe Dayan Center, Tel Aviv University/ Kav Adom, Kibbutz Meuhad Press, 1995.

Enderlin, Charles. *Shattered Dreams: The Failure of the Peace Process in the Middle East, 1995–2002.* New York: Other Press, 2003.

Gelber, Yoav. [Hebrew.] *A Budding Fleur-de-Lis: Israeli Intelligence Services during the War of Independence, 1948–1949.* Tel Aviv: Israel Ministry of Defense, 2000.

———. *Jewish-Transjordanian Relations, 1921–1948.* London: Frank Cass, 1997.

Goren, Arthur, ed. *Dissenter in Zion: From the Writings of Judah L. Magnes.* Cambridge, MA: Harvard University Press, 1982.

Gorenberg, Gershom. *The Accidental Empire: Israel and the Birth of the Settlements, 1967–1977.* New York: Times Books, 2006.

Gresh, Alain. *The PLO: The Struggle Within: Toward an Independent Palestinian State.* London: Zed Books, 1985.

HaCohen, Ran, and Kimmerling, Baruch. [Hebrew.] "A Note on T. Herzl and the Idea of 'Transfer.'" *Yisrael* 6 (Autumn 2004): 163–170.

Hattis, Susan. *The Bi-National Idea on Palestine in Mandatory Times.* Haifa: Shikmona, 1970.

Heller, Yosef. [Hebrew.] *From "Brit Shalom" to "Ihud": Judah Leib Magnes and the Struggle for a Binational State.* Jerusalem: Magnes, 2004.

Herzl, Theodor. *The Complete Diaries of Theodor Herzl.* Edited by Raphael Patai. New York: Herzl Press and T. Yoseloff, 1960.

Judt, Tony. "Israel: The Alternative." *New York Review of Books,* 23 October 2003.

———. "Tony Judt Replies." *New York Review of Books,* 4 December 2003.

Karmi, Ghada. "A Secular Democratic State in Historic Palestine: An Idea Whose Time Has Come?" *Al-Adab* (Lebanon), July 2002.

Katz, Shmuel. [Hebrew.] *Jabo.* Tel Aviv: Dvir, 1993.

Khalidi, Rashid. *The Iron Cage: The Story of the Palestinian Struggle for Statehood.* Boston: Beacon, 2006.

Lazar, Daniel. "The One-State Solution." *Nation,* 3 November 2003.

Magnes, Judah Leib. "Towards Peace in Palestine." *Foreign Affairs,* January 1943.

Mandel, Neville. *The Arabs and Zionism before World War I.* Berkeley: University of California Press, 1980.

Masalha, Nur. *Expulsion of the Palestinians: The Concept of "Transfer" in Zionist Political Thought, 1882–1948.* Washington, DC: Institute for Palestine Studies, 1992.

Mearsheimer, John, and Stephen Walt. *The Israel Lobby and U.S. Foreign Policy.* New York: Farrar, Straus and Giroux, 2007.

Meital, Yoram. "The Khartoum Conference and Egyptian Policy after the 1967 War: A Re-examination." *Middle East Journal* 54 (Winter 2000): 64–82.

Morris, Benny. *The Birth of the Palestinian Refugee Problem Revisited.* Cambridge: Cambridge University Press, 2004.

———. [Hebrew.] "Comment on the Article by Ran HaCohen and Baruch Kimmerling." *Yisrael* 6 (Autumn 2004): 171–173.

———. *1948: A History of the First Arab-Israeli War.* New Haven and London: Yale University Press, 2008.

———. *Righteous Victims: A History of the Zionist-Arab Conflict, 1881–2001.* New York: Vintage Books, 2001.

———. *The Road to Jerusalem: Glubb Pasha, Palestine and the Jews.* London: I. B. Tauris, 2002.

Muslih, Muhammad. *The Origins of Palestinian Nationalism.* New York: Columbia University Press, 1988.

Naor, Arye. [Hebrew.] *Greater Israel: Theology and Policy.* Haifa: Haifa University Press/Zmora-Bitan, 2001.

Nashashibi, Nasser Eddin. *Jerusalem's Other Voice: Ragheb Nashashibi and Moderation in Palestinian Politics, 1920–1948.* Exeter: Ithaca, 1990.

Peretz, Don, *Intifada: The Palestinian Uprising.* Boulder, CO: Westview, 1990.

Porath, Yehoshua. *The Emergence of the Palestinian-Arab National Movement, 1918–1929.* London: Frank Cass, 1974.

———. *The Palestinian Arab National Movement, 1929–1939: From Riots to Rebellion.* London: Frank Cass, 1977.

———. *In Search of Arab Unity, 1930–1945.* London: Frank Cass, 1986.

Ross, Dennis. *The Missing Peace: The Inside Story of the Fight for Middle East Peace.* New York: Farrar, Straus and Giroux, 2004.

Ruppin, Arthur. *Memoirs, Diaries, Letters.* Edited by Alex Bein. London: Weidenfeld and Nicolson, 1971.

Sakakini, Khalil al-. [Hebrew.] *"Such Am I, Oh World!": Diaries of Khalil al-Sakakini.* Jerusalem: Keter, 1990.

Sayigh, Yezid. *Armed Struggle and the Search for State: The Palestinian National Movement, 1949–1993.* Oxford: Oxford University Press, 1997.

Schiff, Ze'ev, and Ehud Ya'ari. *Intifada: The Palestinian Uprising—Israel's Third Front.* New York: Simon and Schuster, 1990.

Shapira, Anita. *Land and Power.* New York: Oxford University Press, 1992.

Shalev, Aryeh. [Hebrew.] *The Intifada: Causes and Effects.* Tel Aviv: Yoffe Center for Strategic Studies/Papyrus, 1990.

Shemesh, Moshe. [Hebrew.] "The Crisis in Palestinian Leadership." *Iyunim Betkumat Yisrael* 14 (2004): 285–335; 15 (2005): 301–348.

Sher, Gilead. [Hebrew.] *Just beyond Reach.* Tel Aviv: Yediot Aharonot/Sifrei Hemed, 2001.

Shlaim, Avi. *Lion of Jordan: The Life of King Hussein in War and Peace.* London: Allen Lane/Penguin, 2007.

Siegman, Henry. "Israel: The Threat from Within." *New York Review of Books,* 26 February 2004.

Sofer, Arnon. "Israel, Demography, 2000–2020: Dangers and Opportunities." Haifa: National Security Studies Center, Haifa University, 2001.

Storrs, Ronald. *Orientations.* London: Ivor Nicholson and Watson, 1937.

Sussman, Gary. "The Challenge to the Two-State Solution." *Middle East Report,* Summer 2004.

Swisher, Clayton. *The Truth about Camp David: The Untold Story about the Collapse of the Middle East Peace Process.* New York: Nation Books, 2004.

Tessler, Mark. *A History of the Israeli-Palestinian Conflict.* Bloomington: Indiana University Press, 1994.

Tilley, Virginia. *The One-State Solution: A Breakthrough for Peace in the Israeli-Palestinian Deadlock.* Manchester: Manchester University Press, 2005.

———. "The One-State Solution." *London Review of Books,* 6 November 2003.

Tsur, Ze'ev. [Hebrew.] *From the Partition Controversy to the Allon Plan.* Israel: Yad Tabenkin, 1982.

Vital, David. *The Origins of Zionism.* Oxford: Oxford University Press, 1975.

Walzer, Michael. Letter to the editor. *New York Review of Books,* 4 December 2003.

Wasserstein, Bernard. *The British in Palestine: The Mandatory Government and the Arab-Jewish Conflict, 1917–1929.* London: Royal Historical Society, 1978.

Weizmann, Chaim. *The Letters and Papers of Chaim Weizmann.* Series A. Vol. 9. Ed. Judah Reinharz. New Brunswick, NJ, and Jerusalem: Transaction Books/Rutgers University Press/Israel Universities Press, 1977.

———. *The Letters and Papers of Chaim Weizmann.* Series A. Vol. 10. Ed. Bernard Wasserstein. New Brunswick, NJ, and Jerusalem: Transaction Books/Rutgers University Press/Israel Universities Press, 1977.

———. *The Letters and Papers of Chaim Weizmann.* Series A. Vol. 14. Ed. Camillo Dresner. New Brunswick, NJ, and Jerusalem: Transaction Books/Rutgers University Press/Israel Universities Press, 1978.

Wieseltier, Leon. "Israel, Palestine and the Return of the Bi-National Fantasy: What Is Not to Be Done." *New Republic,* 27 October 2003.

Zayit, David. [Hebrew.] *Pioneers in the Political Maze: The Kibbutz Movement, 1927–1948.* Jerusalem: Yad Yitzhak Ben-Zvi, 1993.

Index

A Dialogue about the Principal Issues (Khalaf), 117

Aaronsohn, Aaron, 39–40

Abbas, Mahmoud ("Abu Mazen"), 27, 114, 132, 150, 173, 174, 175–176

'Abdullah (prince, later king), 41, 43, 62, 69, 75, 85, 86, 91–92, 99, 100

"Abdulliya," 75

'Abed Rabbo, Yasser, 146, 148, 149

Abraham (patriarch), 74, 81

Abunimah, Ali, 18–20, 219nn2,3

Abu-Sharif, Bassam, 124

Abu-Sitta, Hamid, 122

Abu Sitta, Salman, 204n4

Acre, 31, 52, 122

Aden, 193

Agudat Ihud, 45, 48–50

Ahad Ha'am (Asher Hirsch Ginsberg), 50

Ahdut Ha'avoda Party (movement), 72, 79, 84, 85

Al-Aksa, Mosque, 137

'Alami, Musa al-, 54, 92, 197

Alexander II, 28

Algeria, 181

Allenby, Edmund, 159

Allon, Yigal, 79, 83–86

Allon Plan, 26, 84–87

Almohad dynasty, 192

Alterman, Natan, 82

Amman, 26, 199–200

Anatot, 82

Andalusia, 192

Anglo-American Committee of Inquiry (1946), 96

Annapolis peace conference (2007), 174, 176

Anti-Semitism, 10, 15, 60, 105–106, 121, 156–157, 180, 181–182, 186

Index

Antonius, George, 103–105, 197

Apartheid, 8, 24, 203–204n1

'Aqaba (Eilat), Gulf of, 31, 41, 43, 87, 150

'Araba ('Arava), Wadi, 34, 177

Arab Awakening, The (Antonius), 103–105

Arab Higher Committee (AHC), 53, 98, 100, 102, 182

Arab League, 83, 198

Arab minority (Israel), 24, 69–70, 171, 220–221n18, 222n19

Arab Office, 96

Arab Revolt (1936–1939), 19, 25, 29, 52–54, 60–61, 67, 94, 101, 103, 104

Arab Women's Organization, 109

Arafat, Yasser, 5, 34, 114–115, 117, 118, 119, 120–121, 122, 127–133, 135–140, 149, 150, 164, 166, 167, 170, 171, 172, 173–174, 175, 216n177, 217–218n188, 218n190, 219n5

Ariel, 136

Arlosoroff, Haim, 58

Arnon River, 42

Ashqelon, 164

Atlit, 91, 92

Azoury, Negib, 36–37, 205n9

Baghdad, 29, 42, 103, 192

Bahrain, 193

Balad al-Sheikh, 54

Balfour, Arthur James, 38

Balfour Declaration (1917), 20, 38, 51, 88, 111, 113

Banias Spring (and River), 39

Barak, Ehud, 5, 134–139, 145, 149, 150, 164, 172, 195, 196

Barghouti, Omar Salah, al- 15, 94

Bartov, Omer, 10–11

Basel, 35, 38

Be'ayot Hayom, 49

Bedouin, 8

Beersheba, 31, 122, 204n4

Begin, Menachem, 77, 78, 83, 86, 135, 166

Beirut, 23, 29, 31, 87, 122, 123

Beitar Elit, 71

Beit Shean (Bisan) Valley, 87, 91

Belgium, 187

Ben-'Ami, Shlomo, 135

Ben-Gurion, Amos, 66

Ben-Gurion, David, 9, 40–41, 43, 50, 58, 62, 64, 66–67, 70, 73, 74, 75, 77, 78, 79–80, 83, 107, 197, 211n113

Bentwich, Norman, 93

Ben-Yehuda, Eliezer, 35–36

Ben-Zvi, Yitzhak, 40

Berger, Samuel ("Sandy"), 145

Bergman, Shmuel Hugo, 45

Bernstein, Peretz, 72

Betar movement, 43

Bethel, 73

Bethlehem, 24, 31, 62, 76, 82, 84, 129, 136

Binationalism, 3, 5, 9, 11, 14, 16, 24, 46, 48, 55, 57–60, 89–98, 178, 179, 189, 197

Birth rates, 7–8, 24, 69–70

Blair, Tony, 132

Bludan, 100

British Mandate (Palestine), 18–19, 22, 23, 25, 29, 31, 33, 41, 44, 52, 54, 67–68, 91, 92, 111, 182, 213n140

Brit Shalom, 44–51, 57, 94
Brooks, A. J., 101
Brown, Nathan, 218*nn191,192*
Buber, Martin, 45, 48
Bush, George W., 150, 199

Cadogan, Alexander, 48
Cairo, 29, 83, 174
Camp David Agreements (1978), 166
Camp David talks (2000), 5, 20,
    133–139, 140, 150, 172,
    215–216*n176*, 216*n177*
Canada, 76
Cantonization, 59–60, 91–94
Christian Arabs, 24–25, 52, 88, 107,
    168–169, 184, 191–192
Churchill, Winston, 40–41, 43, 89
City of David, 146
Clinton, Bill, 5, 128, 131, 134–139,
    140–146, 149, 150, 172, 173, 174,
    195, 196, 217*n185*, 218*n190*
Clinton "parameters" (2000), 5, 133,
    140–144, 146–149, 164, 172,
    218*n188*
Coastal Plain, 62, 76, 91, 93
Congo (Belgian), 23
Coupland, Reginald, 63
Crime statistics (Israel), 220–221*n18*
Crusades and crusader kingdoms,
    109, 156, 158–159
Czechoslovakia, 66, 76

Dajani, 'Omar Sidqi al-, 213*n140*
Damascus, 23, 29, 31, 41, 42, 83, 87,
    197
Danzig, 43
Darwish, 'Abd al-Fatah, 53–54
Darwish, Mahmoud, 124

David (king), 39, 81–82
David's Tower, 78
Dayan, Moshe, 70, 81, 83, 86
Dead Sea, 84, 87, 147, 177, 217*n185*
Declaration of Principles (1993), 128
Democratic Front for the Liberation
    of Palestine (DFLP), 169
demography, 23, 46–47, 69–70, 75,
    77, 184–186, 189, 204*n4*
Dichter, Avi, 222*n19*
Dome of the Rock (Mosque of
    'Omar), 137
Dhahiriya, 136
Dubnow, Shimon, 35
Dubnow, Vladimir, 35

East Timor, 23
Edom, 40, 42, 44
Egypt, 8, 16, 32, 45, 69, 74, 81, 83,
    109, 110, 117, 135, 162, 163, 192,
    193, 196
Eilon, Amos, 10
El Arish, 196
Eldad, Yisrael, 74
Electronic Intifada, 18
Elkana, 71
Erikat, Sa'ib, 173, 174
Eshkol, Levi, 80, 82–84, 162
'Etzion Bloc, 84, 136, 141
Euphrates River, 74, 157, 205*n9*

Falastin, 90, 91
Falastin al-Jadida, 94–95
Farmers Association, 48
Fatah, 1, 24, 111, 114–117, 118, 119,
    151, 154, 167, 175, 180
Fatah Constitution (1964), 115–117,
    214*n152*

Fez, 192
France, 11, 33
Freemasons, 157
French Revolution, 157

Galilee, 52, 62, 87, 177, 204*n*4
Galilee (Tiberias), Sea of, 42
Gaza (city), 31, 91, 122–123, 130
Gaza Strip, 2, 5, 7–8, 12, 13, 17,
    21–22, 27, 69–70, 80, 81, 82, 87,
    109, 112, 114, 117, 118, 123, 125,
    126, 128, 135–138, 140, 141, 149,
    152, 153, 154, 160, 162, 163, 164,
    165, 166, 168, 171, 173, 174, 176,
    177, 180, 181, 186, 189, 193,
    194–195, 196, 198–201, 204*n*4,
    218*n*191
General Zionist Party, 72
Geneva, 126
Germany, 23, 45, 60, 66, 104; foreign
    ministry of, 108
Gilead, 40, 42, 44, 73, 78
Golan Heights, 39, 40, 42, 81, 83, 84,
    87, 162
Goldstein, Baruch, 128–129, 151
Good Friday Agreement, 24
Government Arab College, 90
Grady, Henry, 93
Granada, 192
Great Britain (England), 20, 23, 38,
    42, 43, 55, 61, 66, 89, 100, 198;
    foreign office of, 48
"Greater Israel," 72–73, 79, 82–83,
    86, 162, 163
Greece, 63
Greek Catholic Church, 52
Greek-Turkish population transfers
    (1920s), 63–65

Greenberg, Uri Zvi, 73–74
Gresh, Alain, 214*n*161
Guatemala, 76

Hadassah Convoy Ambush/Massacre,
    55
Haganah, 182, 183
Haifa, 18, 54, 88, 91, 177, 180
Haj, 40
Hajjat, Bishop, 52
Hakibbutz Ha'artzi, 56, 57
Hamami, Said, 123
Hamas, 1, 5, 13, 15, 22, 24, 115, 130,
    151, 152, 154–160, 171, 176, 180,
    181, 183, 186, 194, 220*n*9
Hamas Covenant (1988), 154–160
Haniyeh, Ismail, 154, 176
Hapo'el Hatza'ir, 45
Hasbani River, 39
Hashim, Ibrahim, 69
Hashomer Hatza'ir (movement and
    party), 45, 56–58, 94
Hasmoneans, 51
Hassan, Khalid al-, 114, 118, 120
Hattis, Susan, 89
Hebrew University of Jerusalem, 45,
    55, 93
Hebron, 72, 73, 76, 81, 84, 86,
    122–123, 128, 130, 136
Hebron Hills, 78
Hebron Massacre (1929), 19, 47
Herod (king), 40, 51
Herzl, Theodor, 14, 35, 36, 65,
    209*n*71
Hezbollah, 15, 151
Hijaz, 129, 188
Hijaz Railway, 39–40
Hirsch, Sali, 94

Hitler, Adolf, 68, 182
Holland (Netherlands), 76
Holocaust, 25, 29, 75, 108, 183
Holy Basin (*ha'agan hakadosh*), 146
Horan, 41
Horowitz, Joseph, 45
Hourani, Albert, 95–98
Hudnat Hudeibiya, 129
Hussein (king), 85–86, 118, 201
Husseini clan, party, 100–103, 108, 213*n140*
Husseini, Fawzi Darwish al-, 77, 94–95
Husseini, Haj Muhammad Amin al-, 53, 95, 96, 98, 100, 105–109, 110, 118, 150, 166–167, 170, 182
Husseini, Jamal, 93, 95, 98
Husseini, Musa, 107
Husseini, Musa Kazim, 178

Ibn Sa'ud, 'Abd al-'Aziz, 99, 109
Immigration to Palestine/Israel, 89, 104–105; from the former Soviet Union, 71, 185–186; from Muslim countries, 184–185
India, 76
Intifada, First, 123, 155, 163, 198
Intifada, Second, 6, 133, 139–140, 150–152, 154, 173, 203*n1*, 216*n177*
Iran, 10, 15, 76, 222*n20*
Iraq, 25, 32, 61, 65, 74, 99, 107, 183, 193
Iron Cage, The (Khalidi), 3–5, 113–114
Isaac (patriarch), 81
Isdud (Ashdod), 78, 177

Islamic Jihad, 1, 13, 176, 194
Israel Defense Forces (IDF), 78, 81–82, 84, 116, 151, 164, 165, 180
Israel-Jordan General Armistice Agreement (1949), 79
'Iss al-Din al-Qassam brigades, 155
Istanbul (Constantinople), 23, 31, 37
Italy, 61, 73
IZL, 9, 77

Jabotinsky, Ze'ev, 43–44, 73
Jacob (patriarch), 81
Jaffa, 18, 31, 36, 90, 122
Jaffa Muslim-Christian Association, 106
Japan, 23, 61
Jenin, 76, 84, 86, 129, 136
Jeremiah (prophet), 82
Jericho, 85, 128
Jerusalem, 18, 31, 32, 59, 62, 72, 73, 76, 86, 91, 93, 100, 128, 135–136, 142, 147, 165, 172 , 173, 185, 217*n185*
Jerusalem Corridor, 78
Jerusalem District, 23
Jerusalem, East, 3–4, 79, 80, 81, 83, 84, 85, 86, 135, 138, 152, 153, 162, 186, 195, 199, 218*n191;* Armenian Quarter, 138, 149; Christian Quarter, 138, 149; Jewish Quarter, 138; Muslim Quarter, 138, 149
Jewish Agency, 26, 47, 75, 85; Executive, 62, 65, 197; Political Department, 58, 95; Youth Aliya Department, 48
Jewish National Fund (JNF), 67, 72

"Jewish National Home," 38, 39–40, 43, 50, 51, 60, 92, 107

Jewish refugees from Muslim countries, 216–217n183

Jezreel Valley, 76, 87, 91

jihad (holy war), 52, 53, 103, 109, 110, 129, 158

Johannesburg sermon, 129, 172

Jordan (Transjordan), 2, 26, 33, 39, 41–44, 55, 56, 61, 62, 69, 70, 75, 76, 78, 80, 81, 85, 91–92, 103, 109, 118, 162, 177, 196, 198–201

Jordan River, 1, 5, 7, 12, 16, 21–22, 32, 34, 39, 41, 43, 44, 74, 77, 78, 82, 84, 86, 87, 117, 136, 148, 153, 177, 216n177

Jordan Valley, 76, 84–85, 87, 91, 136, 141–142

Joseph's Tomb, 34

Judea, 75, 82, 177

Judean Desert, 87

Jüdische Rundschau, 46

Judt, Tony, 6–14, 18, 220n17

jund falastin, 32, 87

jund urdunn, 87

Kach Party, 70–71

Kaddoumi, Farouk, 131

Kadima Party, 163, 164

Kafr Qassam, 71

Kahane, Meir, 70

Kalak, 'Izz al-Din, 123

Kalvarisky, Haim Margaliyot, 94

Karaoun, Lake, 39

Karbala, 99

Karmi, Ghada, 2–3, 219n3

Karnei Shomron, 71

Katznelson, Berl, 72

Kerak, 41

Khalaf, Salah ("Abu Iyad"), 114, 117, 119, 122, 124

Khalidi, Ahmed, 90–92, 211n113

Khalidi, Rashid, 3–5, 113–114, 167–168, 219n3

Khalidi, Yusuf Diya al-, 33

Khan, Zadok, 33

Khartoum Summit and resolutions (1967), 83, 86, 122, 211n102

King-Crane Commission (1919), 106

Kisch, Frederick, 65

Knesset, 45, 183

Lazar, Daniel, 14–15

League for Arab-Jewish Rapprochement and Cooperation, 94–95

League of Nations, 22, 23, 41, 65, 208n68

Lebanese civil war (1975–1990), 121

Lebanon, 2, 31, 33, 34, 39, 55, 69, 109, 114, 123, 177, 195, 204n4

LHI, 9, 74, 183

Libya, 122

Lieberman, Avigdor, 71

Lions Club, 157

Litani River, 31, 34, 39–40, 177

Lloyd George, David, 38

London Conference, 108

London Review of Books, 16–17

Lydda, 78

Ma'ale Adumim, 136, 216n177

Ma'an, 41

Macedonia, 63

Index

Magnes, Judah Leib, 45, 48–56, 62, 74, 77, 91, 94, 95, 96, 98, 197
Mahkame, 146
Majdal (Ashqelon), 78
Manchester Guardian, 101
Mapai (later Labor Party or Alignment), 62, 72, 79, 85, 86, 127, 163, 164, 185, 199
Mashal, Khalid, 176
Mash'al, Sharif ("Abu Zaki"), 175
Mishmar Ha'emeq, 57
Moab, 40, 42, 44
Moledet Party, 70–71
Morocco, 192, 193
Morrison, Herbert, 93
Morrison-Grady Plan (1946), 93
Motzkin, Leo, 65
Mount of Olives, 146
Mughannam, Matiel, 108–109
Muhammad (prophet), 129, 158–159
Muslim Brotherhood, 154–155
Mussolini, Benito, 59
Myerson (Meir), Golda, 75, 86, 162

Nablus (Shechem), 32, 34, 53, 76, 81, 84, 129, 136, 180
Najaf, 99
Nashashibi clan, party (Opposition), 94, 100, 101–103
Nashashibi, Fakhri al-, 103
Nashashibi, Nasser Eddin, 102, 212n131
Nashashibi, Ragheb, 100, 101–103, 212n131, 212–213n132
Nation, 14
National Defense Party, 100, 102, 212n131

National Religious Party (NRP), 85, 134
Nazis, National Socialism, 181–183
Negev (Neqeb or Naqb) Desert, 42, 43, 78, 87, 94
Netanyahu, Benjamin, 130–132, 134
New Republic, 12–13
New York Review of Books, 6, 10, 12
New York Times, 77
Nile River, 74, 157, 205n9
9/11, 6
1920 riots, 19
1921 riots, 19
1929 riots, 19, 47
1948 War, 9, 21, 25, 69–70, 78–79, 84, 109, 116, 143, 162, 179, 188, 204n4
1956 (Sinai/Suez) War, 80–81
1967 (Six Day) War, 70, 80, 81, 84, 112, 116, 162, 179
1973 (Yom Kippur or October) War, 117, 118
1982 (Lebanon) War, 123
Northern Ireland, 24
Norway, 127

Ofel Garden, 146
Olmert, Ehud, 199
One Country: A Bold Proposal to End the Israeli-Palestinian Impasse (Abunimah), 18–20, 168
One-State Solution: A Breakthrough for Peace in the Israeli-Palestinian Deadlock, The (Tilley), 17–18, 179–184
Orientations, 59
Ormsby-Gore, William, 178

Oslo Accord, peace process (1990s), 7, 128, 129, 130, 171, 172

Ottoman Empire, 23, 29, 31–32, 34, 36, 37, 41, 87

Ottoman parliament, 102

Oxford University, 96

Palestine Arab Congress, Third (1920), 88

Palestine Arab Executive, 178

Palestine Liberation Organisation (PLO), 1, 2, 5, 34, 85, 110–113, 115, 117, 118, 119, 120, 121, 122, 123, 124, 125, 126–132, 149, 151, 159, 164, 167, 168, 169–170, 171, 172, 175, 183, 201, 204n4, 214n161

Palestine National Authority or Palestinian Authority (PNA or PA), 22, 27, 34, 129, 130–131, 140, 143, 146, 148, 149, 151, 152, 153, 154, 174, 175, 194, 199–201

Palestine National Council (PNC), 108, 110, 112, 114, 118–119, 124, 125, 126, 127–128, 130, 132, 133, 154, 168, 169, 171, 214n161, 219n3

Palestinian Arab refugee problem, 25, 128, 137–139, 143–144, 146, 147, 166, 173, 199–200, 204n4

Palestinian Declaration of Independence (1988), 124, 154

Palestinian National Covenant (or Charter) (1964), 1, 108, 110–113, 121, 127–128, 130–132, 167, 168

Peel, Lord William Robert Wellesley, 178, 213n143

Peel Commission, 52, 59–60, 66, 67, 68, 85, 98, 102, 104, 106, 178, 190–191

Peel Commission Report (proposals), 61–64, 66, 72, 73, 74, 93, 99, 100, 102, 103–104, 133–134

Peres, Shimon, 86, 130, 162

Peru, 76

Piedmont, 73

Plutzker, Sever, 203–204n1

Po'alei Zion Party, 94

Poland, 10, 66

Popular Front for the Liberation of Palestine (PFLP), 122

Porath, Yehoshua, 197

Price, J. S., 53

"Protocols of the Elders of Zion, The," 156

Qalqilya, 76, 86

Quartet, 152

Qurai, Suleiman Ahmed ("Abu Alaa"), 173

Quraish tribe, 129

Quran (Koran), 53, 106, 155, 158

Rabin, Yitzhak, 86, 127–128, 130, 132, 139, 162, 163

Rafah, 40–41, 117

Ramallah, 31, 76, 78, 84, 86, 129, 136, 176, 180

Ramla, 62, 78, 87

Ras al-Naqura (Naqura), 117

Rendel, George, 208–209n68

Reveil de la nation arabe dans l'Asie turque, Le (Azoury), 37

Revisionist Movement (Herut Party, later Gahal, later Likud), 43–44, 73, 77, 79, 85–86, 130, 139, 162–163, 164, 185
Risorgimento, 73
Romania, 12
Rosen (Rosenblueth), Pinhas (Felix), 45
Ross, Dennis, 135, 138, 146, 148, 217n187
Rotary Club, 157
Ruppin, Arthur, 45–48, 51, 65
Russia, 152
Russian Revolution, 157

Sadat, Anwar, 117, 122, 135, 166
Said, Edward, 16, 124
Sa'id, Nuri, 54, 68
Sakakini, Khalil al-, 33
Saladin, 158
Samaria, 52, 82, 177
Samuel, Herbert, 197
Sapir, Pinhas, 83
Sartawi, Issam, 123
Sasson, Elias (Eliahu), 75
Saudi Arabia, 10, 99
Sayigh, Yezid, 115, 120
Sderot, 164
"secular democratic state," 2–3, 5, 113, 153, 167–171, 219n3
Sephardim, 184–185
Serbia, 10
settlements and settlers, 8, 17, 19–20, 83–84, 128, 163
Sha'at, Nabil, 152, 173
Shamir, Moshe, 82
Sharett (Shertok), Moshe, 80

Shari'a, 218n192
Sharon, Ariel ("Arik"), 13, 139–140, 150, 151
Shas Party, 134
Sher, Gilead, 135, 145
Shin Bet (Israel's General Security Service), 181
Shukeiry, Ahmed, 110
Sidon, 40
Siegman, Henry, 219–220n9
Simon, Akiba Ernst, 47, 48, 94
Sinai Peninsula, 80–81, 83, 135, 150, 162, 163
Smilansky, Moshe, 48
Sofer, Arnon, 7
Solomon (king), 40, 74
South Africa, 4, 10, 17, 24, 129, 203–204n1
South Wall, 146
Soviet Union, 77, 115, 185, 198
Spain, 192
Sprinzak, Yosef, 45
Storrs, Ronald, 59
Sudan, 190
Suez Canal, 61
Sulaiman, Hikmat, 99
Supreme Muslim Council, 182
Sussman, Gary, 15–16
Sweden, 76
Switzerland, 35
Sykes-Picot Agreement (1916), 149, 218n189
Syria, 2, 10, 29, 32–33, 55, 69, 81, 83, 88, 109, 111, 114, 121, 122, 177, 190, 193, 195
Syrian Desert, 41
Szold, Henrietta, 48

Taba talks, 150
Tabenkin, Yitzhak, 72–73
Taibe, 71
Tel Aviv, 77, 91, 92, 165, 180
Temple, First, 39, 82, 143
Temple, Second, 39, 82, 143
Temple Mount (*har habayit* or *al-Haram al-Sharif*), 137–140, 142–143, 145, 147–148, 150, 173
Thessaly, 63
Thon, Jacob, 45
Tiberias, 87
Tilley, Virginia, 16–18, 179–184
Time, 219n5
Times (London), 100
Tolkowsky, Shmuel, 39–40
Tomb of the Patriarchs (al-Ibrahimiyya Mosque), 128, 151
Tombs of the Kings and Prophets, 146
Transfer, 63–70, 71–72, 209n74
Tripoli (Libya), 122
Truman, Harry, 109
Tulkarm, 76, 86, 129
Tunis, 123, 129, 131
Turkey, 8, 63
Tyre, 40

'Udwan, Kamal, 117
Uj River, al-, 40
Ultra-Orthodox and Orthodox Jews, 185, 193
Umm al-Fahm, 71
United Nations, 22, 23, 152, 153, 157, 204n4; General Assembly, 76, 120–121, 126, 219n5; Secretariat, 76

United Nations General Assembly (Partition) Resolution 181, 5, 69, 77, 78, 80, 123, 124–125, 133–134, 162
United Nations General Assembly Resolution 194, 144
United Nations Security Council, 157; Resolution 242, 122, 126, 127; Resolution 338, 122, 126, 127
United Nations Special Committee on Palestine (UNSCOP) (1947), 76, 96
United States, 13, 15, 55, 56, 83, 126, 127, 131, 134, 139, 147, 152, 183–184, 190
Uruguay, 76
Ussishkin, Menahem, 65, 72

Versailles Peace Conference (1919), 38, 64
Vienna, 46, 56

Wahida, Al, 108
Wailing (Western) Wall, 138, 142–143, 145–146, 217n187
Walzer, Michael, 11–12
Washington, DC, 13, 27
Wazzani River, 39
Weizmann, Chaim, 38–41, 58, 62, 65, 68
Weltsch, Robert, 46
West Bank, 2, 3–4, 7–8, 21–22, 24, 26, 27, 69–70, 71, 75, 76, 78, 79, 80, 81, 83, 84–86, 91, 109, 112, 117, 118, 123, 125, 126, 128, 129, 135–138, 140, 141, 142, 147, 149, 151, 152, 153, 154, 162, 163, 164,

West Bank (continued)
  165, 166, 171, 173, 174, 177, 181,
  185, 189, 193, 194, 195, 196,
  198–201, 217*n185*, 218*n191*
Western Wall Tunnel, 146
White paper of 1922 (Churchill), 42
White paper of 1939 (MacDonald),
  63
Wieseltier, Leon, 12–13
Wilkansky, Yitzhak Avigdor, 209*n74*
World War I (1914–1918), 29–30, 33,
  38, 107–108, 157, 159
World War II (1939–1945), 29, 48,
  49, 55, 57, 58, 66, 108, 158, 197

Ya'ari, Meir, 56
Yaboq (Jabbok) River, 39, 42

Yarmuk River, 39, 42
Yassin, Ahmed, 154, 220*n9*
Yemen, 123, 190
Yisrael Ba'aliya Party, 134
Yisrael Beiteinu Party, 71–72
Yugoslavia, 76
Yugoslav wars (1990s), 6, 11

Ze'evi, Rehav'am ("Gandhi"), 71
Zimbabwe, 10
Zionist Congress, First (1897), 35, 36
Zionist Congress, Seventeenth
  (1931), 44, 46
Zionist Congress, Twentieth (1937),
  62, 64, 66–67
Zionist Organisation, 29, 45, 57
Zurich, 66